CW00524408

THE ULTIMATE GUI.
SUCCESSFUL

BY CATHERINE BALAVAGE

First published in January 2016

Copyright © Catherine Balavage 2016

ISBN 978-0-9929639-9-6

For my son Luke: you are all my dreams come true

THE ULTIMATE GUIDE TO BECOMING A SUCCESSFUL BLOGGER

The Ultimate Guide To Becoming a Successful Blogger

Introduction.

Chapter 1: Getting Started. Design, Choosing a Name And The Benefits of Blogging.

Chapter 2: Revenue Streams. The Different Options And How To Make Money

Chapter 3: Content. What To Write About And Giving Readers What They Want

Chapter 4: Media. Pictures And Video

Chapter 5: Working With PR People

Chapter 6: Promoting and Marketing Your Blog.

Chapter 7: SEO And Other Growth Strategy

Chapter 8: Social Media

Chapter 9: Further Tips For Building Your Blog

Chapter 10: Interviews

INTRODUCTION.

Blogging has exploded in the past few years. It seems that everyone these days is a blogger and many have fantasies of giving up their day job to blog full time. While many people have blogs, only a few actually make a full-time living from it. The truth is, it is possible to earn a living as a blogger but it takes a lot of hard work.

This is an achievement but one that can be attained. The internet has, in many ways, made the world more democratic. It used to take decades to become a brand, now that can happen in years, sometimes less. Things can take off quickly but not without knowledge and hard work. That is why I wrote this book. I want to give you that knowledge. I started Frost Magazine in 2010. In six years I have learned a lot and have built a blog that is read all over the world. I have over 100 writers and amazing editors, all entertaining our readers. Thanks to Frost I have been on all-inclusive press trips abroad, reviewed a significant number of the top restaurants in London, been to London Fashion Week, the Sundance Film Festival, the London Film Festival and every other event that is worth going to. I have met people and done things I would never have been able to do otherwise. My writers and I review everything from wine to chocolate, to clothes and the latest technology. It is not just a blog: it's a lifestyle. I also make enough money from Frost, and the opportunities it gives me, to work from home and earn a living as a self-employed freelancer. In short: it gives me freedom. Frost is the best decision I ever made in my life. I hope, with the help of this book, your blog can become one of the greatest decisions you ever made too. Even if you want to start a blog just to promote yourself or your business, it is an excellent idea. Blogs are the new business cards. Everyone should have one. In a competitive world, standing out is important. Blogging is also amazing because you can write about what you want as long as you don't libel someone. You have freedom, editorial freedom. It is a beautiful thing.

It takes a lot of work to make a blog successful. Blogging may give you the freedom to be your own boss and set your own hours. It even allows you to work from home and spend time with your family. However, if you want to make easy money, go and do something else because blogging is hard work and you have to constantly put more work in. There will be days where it is almost impossible to motivate yourself but you have to, somehow, work up the energy to write a blog post and answer hundreds of emails. It can be tough but it is completely worth it. There is no greater feeling than when all of that hard work pays off. Add in the fact that you are your own boss and can work anywhere in the world as long as you have a computer and an internet connection, you are one lucky person indeed. But luck requires hard work. So let's get started.

I am going to make a number of assumptions before we carry on. I am going to assume you know what a blog is but here is a little on how a blog is different from a normal website.

The difference between a normal website and a blog are the following things: A blog gets updated regularly, a blog will have an archive set by dates, either monthly or yearly, a blog will be updated chronologically; newest posts at the top, oldest posts at the bottom. Tags/categories: a blog will have tags or categories, where certain keywords have been put into a post so search engines can find them and that you can click on the tags/categories and get other posts in that category. Blogs also encourage comments. Some blogs also have a blogroll which is a list of other blogs that they like and an RSS feed which stands for Really Simple Syndication. This allows readers to subscribe and get updates on your blog as a feed and they don't even need to visit your blog. A blog is simply a 'web log'. This means it is a regularly updated site about news/events or ideas,

You may notice that when I talk about a successful blog I talk about more than money. Blogging can give you fame, a voice, respect in your own industry, attention, applause. Having a blog means you can make a name for yourself. You can communicate and connect with people.

Chapter 1: Getting Started. Design, Choosing a Name And The Benefits of Blogging.

I am going to assume that you already know what a blog is, that you probably already have one and that you have a basic understanding of blogging. This won't be an overtly technical book but, to avoid disappointment, and help you along if you are at the very beginning, I have covered the basics of setting one up.

This book will be mostly focused on growing a blog and turning it into a success. Any technical stuff not covered should be on a wonderful place called the internet, so get Googling. The blogging community is also great and very supportive, so don't be scared to join forums or ask anyone any more questions. I hope this book helps you grow your brand and your blog to the next level. It is all achievable with the knowledge and hard work. Growing a blog is about running a business and growing a brand.

Success means different things to different people. It could mean fame, money, prestige, influence … anything you want. But whatever it is that you want it will be a lot of hard work. That doesn't mean it won't be achievable however. Here is how.

The Benefits of Blogging

The benefits of blogging are many. You can work absolutely anywhere in the world as long as you have a computer and an internet connection. You can even blog using your phone. If you are a parent you can stay at home with your children whilst also working and making money. You get to do the things you love and then write about them. To make money doing something you love is a privilege most people don't get. It will be your business that you built up from the ground.

There are also negatives of course. Blogs need constant work if they are to be successful. You can't just tale a two week holiday, you would have to schedule two-week's worth of articles before you go. For me, the benefits vastly outweigh the negatives. I hope they do for you too.

SETTING UP YOUR BLOG

There are a number of options when it comes to setting up a blog. It may take about five minutes to set up a blog (yes, really) but choose your platform carefully. There are a number to choose from and different ones suit different people. You could change your platform later but it will be tricky technically and might cost money.

Hosted platforms (where your site will be hosted on someone else's server. In the book this will be called self-hosting although you will be paying to have your site hosted on a company's server). All offer a range of services and self-installed software ranging in price. Some are free although you will have to pay for the hosting and the domain name, paying for the blog software is optional. It is easy to install, usually just the press of a button and then you need to choose a theme. There are plenty of free ones to get you started or you can choose a premium one that you pay for. If you choose WordPress it is just a case of going through the themes and choosing one.

Of course you can use a free WordPress account but it doesn't look very professional and does not allow advertising so keep that in mind. You can upgrade later but your options may still be limited, but not if you choose a hosting company and then use WordPress as a template to build your site. After you have chosen a WordPress theme you can tweak it and change things to personalise it to your blog. I have used WordPress as a platform for Frost for five years now. I have changed the template a few times but have never had a major problem with it. WordPress is very easy to use.

You can use both WordPress or Blogger for free. They both offer an all-inclusive package which includes the platform, hosting and a web address. The web address will end with WordPress.com and the Blogger one with blogspot.com. To be honest this does not look professional and if you are serious about your blog you should avoid this. My acting blog is a free WordPress blog. I have no complaints but I feel if Frost was the same it would put some people, and advertisers, off. Another option is TypePad which offers a similar service. It charges a monthly fee but has more options for customisation. The Huffington Post uses TypePad.

You can also self-host your blog. Just buy a hosting package via a hosting company like Bluehost or GoDaddy. You can also buy your domain name through these companies. You can then download software to build your site that you have to download and then install yourself. This sounds harder than it is. A lot of hosting companies will just have an 'install Wordpress' button and then you are on your way. I have always found hosting companies very helpful and always willing to offer technical support. Check the customer reviews of any hosting site that you are thinking of choosing. Have a good look at what other people are using and ask around for recommendations. Most people are happy to share their experience and give tips.

Keep in mind how technical you are, and how technical you will be in the future. WordPress is easy but coding your own site would obviously be much harder. If you are not technical, and never will be, then go for the easy option, unless you are prepared to pay someone to help out. If you are technically hopeless then remember that there is a huge, supportive, blogging community out there and lots of forums. You won't be alone. Crying and overwhelmed, but not alone.

WHAT IS THE DIFFERENCE BETWEEN AN ONLINE MAGAZINE AND A BLOG?

I call Frost 'Frost Magazine' although it is technically also a blog. A magazine is a publication that contains essays, stories and articles by a variety of writers. It also contains pictures and tends to specialise in a particular subject or area. So you can use either/or. Frost also has an e-edition. The difference between an online magazine and a blog is also about style and editorial content. Your site can be a blog or an online magazine. It is up to you.

CHOOSING A NAME

Choosing a name can be hard, mostly because most names are taken. Trying to find something original and good which has not already been taken is difficult. The name you choose should reflect your blog. If the blog name relates to your blog niche it will also help with Search Engine Optimisation. You cannot have the same domain name as someone else and you wouldn't want to as this would confuse readers and your brand. Frost Magazine is so called because all of the other domain names that were tried were taken. Well, that and the fact it just sounded good and was memorable. If you have a beauty blog having something related to beauty in the title will let people know what it is about and help SEO, but if you want to change your blog niche, or branch into other topics this might confuse your branding. Weigh up the benefits of having useful keywords in the title to having a memorable name that sticks in people's minds. Do not choose a domain name that is time-specific however. The internet moves fast and anything that ages you will only hurt your brand.

Short domain names are generally better than long ones. They are easier to remember and type out. When it comes to what to have after the dot, it is best to go for .com first. Unless you are trying to target a specific organisation or country (co.uk for example). The letters at the end of your URL are called TDLs which stand for Top Level Domains. There are two types, ones based on country (,fr, .co.uk) and then the generic ones that point to a certain organisation. Governments generally have .org whilst education blogs tend to have .edu.

Other points to remember are any legal ramifications. Make sure your domain name is original and not copyrighted or used by anyone else. You don't want to get into any expensive legal battles or be forced to change your name after you have already gotten started. Think carefully before adding 'blog' to the domain name that you choose. Unfortunately, there is still a stigma from traditional publishers and PR people towards blogs.. I called Frost 'Frost Magazine' because it is run like an online magazine and has a monthly e-edition too. I believe this helped give it credibility in the beginning. Blogs are the way forward and great things, unfortunately some dinosaurs and snobs cannot see this yet.

Another thing to consider is getting the co.uk and other TDLs of your blog name. This means no one else will be able to buy it and it protects your brand.

If you are unsure about whether or not the blog name is any good then ask trusted family and friends for their opinion. They might have valuable opinions. One more thing to look out for is if the domain has been used before. Spammers will sometimes buy a domain and then abandon it. The domain name will be known as a spam blog by some people and banned by Google. Not a good start. On the other hand, maybe someone used it and it has a lot of positive links already pointing its way. Either way, do your research.

If you find your site is banned or has any problems these can be sorted out through Google Webmaster Tools at https://www.google.com/webmasters/tools/home

Make sure the name suits the tone of the blog. It will be easier to sell your blog if your own name is not in it. Arianna Huffington is the exception to the rule, but she is still involved with The Huffington Post after selling it to AOL for hundreds of millions of pounds. Don't include dates. All dates do is date you.

Buy the other endings for your URL. (co.uk, .gov). This protects your brand and stops other people riding on your success or stealing your traffic. The more domain endings you have the more money you will pay but it is worth investing in.

If you are really struggling to find a name there are name generator programmes on the internet that you can use. It would be great if your blog subject matches your name.

BUYING A DOMAIN AND HOSTING.

When you buy a domain name, depending on the company you go with, you will also be given an email address with the domain name in. yourname@domainname.com. I have some of these for Frost. They are easy to set up and look more professional. I also set up one for writers who want one. It looks better when they are contacting PR people. You might get some free with your hosting but they will have a small amount of storage and you will probably have to pay out more money if you want more gigabytes. I also use a gmail account just because it is easier and the emails go straight to my iPhone and can be easily accessed anywhere. You can get a domain from your hosting company or a site like 123-reg.co.uk. Just put 'buy a domain' into Google. Job done. They are very easy to buy. If you choose a separate domain company from the hosting company that you go for then you will have to point the domain to your web host, Check with the hosting company for how to do this. Hosting companies are (usually) great with technical support.

Self-hosting gives you more freedom and full control of your own blog. There are a lot of plugins made by great developers that can also add to your blog. Platforms other than WordPress also have developers making add-ons. Having your own URL (Uniform Resource locator) makes you look more professional and makes it easier to market your brand as it is easier to remember. Although you will pay for the hosting and domain name, running WordPress or another platform is usually free. There may be better designs that you can buy, these are not usually that expensive and the fee is a one-off.

I always recommend WordPress self-hosting. WordPress is the industry standard and having a .com rather than wordpress.com or blogspot.com etc., will make your blog look much more professional. WordPress is the industry standard and there will be a lot of people who just won't take you seriously without a self-hosted domain.

Although it is reasonably easy to set up a self-hosted blog, it can seem daunting. If you are completely non-technical you may find it hard but getting a friend to help, or reading up on the many forums can help you on your way. While self-hosting can start off cheaply (yearly fees for domain name, a registration fee for the domain name and hosting), as your blog becomes more popular the hosting can become expensive. As your traffic increases you might need to move to a bigger package. This has happened a few times with Frost and it is very stressful. Always negotiate with the hosting company rather than just agreeing to pay more money. You may even find it is a plugin or a lot of media that is putting the price up, not the traffic. Always check before parting with your money.

With self-hosting you completely own your blog and are free to sell it. Most professional blogs are self-hosted. There are a few that are not but not many. Self-hosting looks much more professional and some people will think your blog is less professional if it is hosted on WordPress or another free platform. A hosted blog will also restrict the income you can earn from your blog.

Tip - Back up. Pay extra for backing up if you need to. Not losing all of your hard work is the most important thing.

If you have some money and want to invest in your blog, or it has been going for a while and you want it to look more slick and professional, then you can pay for someone to custom design it. Don't panic if you don't have the money, however, a self-hosted, WordPress blog can look as professional as any other blog.

A self-hosted blog will be easy to set up. Just choose your provider and then follow the instructions. Then just click the 'install WordPress' (or any other chosen platform) button. These are usually one-click installs. You can also get your domain from the hosting company. It all sounds complicated and scary if you are not technical but, trust me, I was not technical and it is all very easy to do. Signing up for a free WordPress account is also just as easy. If you can set up an email account, you can set up a blog.

Make sure your site looks personal, something that draws people in. Be clear that there is a real person behind your blog.

Have a headshot in a prominent place above the fold, make sure the 'about' page is easy to find. Make sure your personality comes across and that you explain what the blog and brand is about. This is Frost's about' page (http://www.frostmagazine.com/about-us/) We also have a Frost Magazine Team page where people can learn more about the writers and relate to them. (http://www.frostmagazine.com/the-frost-magazine-team/)

Highlight popular posts. You can do this in the sidebar. It will make new visitors keep reading if you make some images to highlight the good content or have a top posts list in the side bar.

THEMES AND PLUGINS

I know I am sounding like an ambassador for WordPress at this point but another reason to go with them is not only because it is easy to choose a theme and then just click to highlight the good content, or have a top post plugins that developers make that add greatly to your blog, and all you have to do to install them is search for the topic you want (SEO for example) and then click and install your chosen plugin. Each plugin generally gets reviewed by others in the WordPress community and are allocated stars. Four or five stars is always good. You can install plugins by downloading ZIP files, uncompressing the files the ZIP file contains and then uploading them to the appropriate directory by using FTP. You would then activate them by going to the plugin menu. Plugins would be uploaded to the wp-content/plugins directory if you are using WordPress. I have never done this myself and this is not an overtly technical book so I will leave it there. Luckily you don't have to do this for most plugins on a self-hosted WordPress blog. You just have to activate them and change some settings at most. Phew.

For themes: WordPress.org/extend/themes

For plugins: codex.WordPress.org/plugins

Tip- Put a contact form on your website so people can reach you.

PRESENTATION

Put time and effort into your design. The better and more professional you make your blog look the more you will be taken seriously. We live in a visual world and a good design will draw people in, whereas a bad design may put people off, no matter how good your content is. Have a look at other blogs to get some ideas. Make sure it suits your content, theme and personal style. As you learn more you can give it tweaks here and there, or even a full makeover. I have done this a few times. Sometimes it is good to keep updating and give people something new.

When thinking about your blog design think about your audience. If you want to write a business blog then having a pink, frilly background won't attract the right kind of people. Always think about your audience. What you will need on your blog are contact details, an about page, advertising, recent blog list, blog roll (optional), newsletter sign up, social media: Twitter, Facebook, Instagram etc., subscription buttons, logo, search bar and archives.

Think about the colour of your blog. Different colours mean different things and create different moods. Go through options in themes and choose different colours and fonts. Think about your header image and other design features.

If you want a coder (someone who will write computer code for you) then try this site: rentacoder.com

When changing code on your blog ALWAYS copy and paste it to a separate document beforehand. This will stop you breaking your entire site just trying to make a slight change.

You can find all of the different HTML codes for colour here: http://www.w3schools.com/html/html_colors.asp

If you really want to be a hardcore blogger you could always learn how to code. It is a very popular thing to do now and will greatly add to your CV. Coding is a huge plus, as is the ability to sort out any technical issues that may arise. I have relied on some wonderful friends to help with the technical side of my site and also my marketing agency, Handpicked Collective. Funnily enough, I am now quite technical, but only because I have had to be. In the beginning I was hopeless.

Starting any business is scary but the beauty of online is that the startup costs are small. You can buy web-hosting and a domain name for less than £100. The first year of Frost the web hosting cost $100 (we paid in dollars as it was an American company), and we made that back with advertising. How many businesses break even in their first year? Not many. But you will also be spending a significant amount of time on your blog, and those hours will be unpaid initially. So make sure this is something that you really want to do.

CHOOSING A PLATFORM.

WORDPRESS

I use a WordPress template for Frost. Frost is not hosted by WordPress, I just use their software as a template. This makes updating the blog and making technical changes very easy. Many people have asked me who does the web design for Frost or think I am very technical but I am not. There is no coding. It is very easy and it can also look very professional.

According to Wikipedia, 9 out of the top 20 blogs in the world use WordPress. Even the amazing Mashable uses WordPress. As do techcrunch.com and TMZ.com.

WordPress is used by 22% of the top 10 million websites as of 2013 according to Wikipedia. It is the most popular blogging platform. You don't need coding ability for WordPress, you just need to sign up and then do some tweaks. There are also a lot of great free plugins and themes for WordPress.

If you sign up to wordress.com then you get a blog on their servers. You only want this to test WordPress or for a personal blog you don't want to advertise on wordpress.com is different, you download the software to use on your own server. Always opt for the latter when professionally blogging. Most hosting companies offer one click WordPress installation. I would factor this in when choosing one. It is so much easier and will save a lot of stress. I use bluehost.com

If you are good at programming you can use the standard theme on WordPress and then make your own changes by editing the files at wp/content/themes/[name-of-your-theme] folder.

Make sure you choose a theme with a font that is easy to read. The layout should not be too cluttered. Make sure the content is the main attraction and you don't have too many widgets. There should be nothing flashing. To install a theme from WordPress go to Appearance- Themes- Install Themes. You can then upload the theme file or install the theme from there. Most themes, particularly the free ones, allow you to install with a click of a button and even allow you to preview the theme to see what it would look like. Very handy. WordPress is great because basically it works straight out of the box.

Codementor. Although WordPress is free and easy to use you may need some technical help sometimes. If so then there is an online marketplace called Codementor. Codementor connects you to expert developers through a live video call. It is very easy to use as you just enter what you need help with and then you get matched with a developer. It doesn't take long to find someone and the rates are very low. Definitely worth looking into.

GOOD PLUGINS.

- Contact Form 7 (lets you put a contact form on your site)
- Subscribe to comments (lets readers subscribe to comments so they get notified when other people comment on the same article)
- Widget Logic (allows you to only have certain widgets on certain pages. Handy)
- All in one SEO pack (optimise pages and posts for search engines)
- Relates Posts Slider (a slider of related posts so readers can find your other amazing articles)
- Sharebar (Lets you add social sharing buttons.)
- W3 Total Cache (caches plugins to reduce server overload and make sure your site runs smoothly)
- Akismet (this is great because it protects your blog from spam)

To add plugins to your blog go to your WordPress dashboard. Go to Plugins- Add New and then search which plugin or type of plugin you want to use. All you have to do after that is click install and then activate. Job done.

Feedburner is a subscription tool which is owned by Google. It is easy to use. Get it at feedburner.com and then go to publicise- email subscriptions and then click activate. Select the code and then copy it. Then go to WordPress and click Appearances and then click on Widgets. Drag a text box widget into the sidebar and then paste the code into the box. Click save. Done. You can give the widget a title and then there may be some configuration but don't worry as any configuration will be relatively simple. Next time you post a new article the subscribers will be informed.

Always take care of your data. Always make sure that you back up and that if you don't self-host that you have a copy of your data in case the business that hosts your data goes bust. Your data is your business, look after it.

BLOGGER

Blogger is a hosting platform which is very popular with bloggers. I have had a go at using it and it is easy and simple. You just set up an account and then publishing your posts is easy. The only downside is that it can look unprofessional, or like a million other blogs out there. It will definitely look like a blog and maybe not as slick or as glamorous as it could be.

Whilst Blogger is popular for bloggers it does not look as professional as WordPress in my opinion. It also puts limits on your blog while using WordPress doesn't.

Make sure you have 100% control of your blog. My advice is not go with a free blog if you want to make money and treat it like a business.

Self-hosting may also mean you get your own email address with the same URL as your blog. Not all packages offer this for free however. Some will charge you a bit more.

Think about the bandwidth you get when choosing a self-hosting company. You don't want to build your blog and get a lot of traffic only for them to pull you blog or reduce your bandwidth because you are using too much. When you pay for self-hosting you will be on a server with other websites unless you pay a premium. This means that if you use too much the self-hosting company might even stop hosting your site. This is a nightmare and do not take it quietly. Complain and tell them that it is not okay. Also make sure that you don't get screwed over moving to a much more expensive plan when you are not using that much bandwidth at all. Some companies will do this, in fact, when I started blogging, some hosting companies tried to do that to me. Negotiate hard.

When you look for a self-hosting deal look for good data space and bandwidth. Also consider technical support. This is very important. If your blog goes down you lose advertising revenue and readers. If you are going to be uploading lots of pictures and video then think about how much disk space you will need. Check what you are getting and always shop around.

CHECKLIST

- Take a basic programming course. It will really help.

- Make sure people can comment on your blog.

- Make sure it is easy to contact you.

- There should be space for advertising.

- Trademark your site. Seek legal advice.

- Choose what you want to write about.

Create new and unique content.

Deciding what to write about. Find a subject. Make sure you care about the subject you are writing about. Otherwise it will come across to the reader. Think about what you enjoy reading, this will let you know what you will enjoy writing about. What section of WH Smiths do you spend most of your time in?

Subjects you can choose include: fashion, sport, beauty, politics, parenting, food, technology or even a mix of any of the above. You don't need to choose one thing, just make sure you choose subjects you will continue to write about and feel passion for..

Always analyse the market and keep long term growth in mind. You need a business plan.

Don't worry too much about a saturated market as long as you have something to offer. Just be unique. Food blogger Deliciously Ella has become hugely successful even though there are a large number of food bloggers out there, millions even. She was unique because she had been ill and had made herself healthy through learning about nutrition and cooking. Her food is gluten and dairy free and vegan. She has created a niche for herself within her subject. All of the mainstream media she got helped too. She now has her own cookbook, creates recipes for Waitrose and has an app for her blog which made a lot of money.

Be unique; don't just rehash the same content everyone else is doing. Give people stuff they won't be able to get anywhere else.

Until you become successful you can buy tickets to events like the BAFTAS and the Brits. Many stars spend a long time talking to fans and you could get a good scoop. You could also sneak backstage or into the VIP area. Interview people yourself and ask them fresh questions. Write about what you are wearing and take pictures.

Break stories before anyone else. Build rapport with successful people. Use better pictures. Get exclusive interviews.

BE CURRENT AND RELEVANT.

Engage with your readers. Respond to them on social media; ask questions at the bottom of articles to encourage comments. Always reply to comments. Make your readers feel like they are part of a community. Mix it up, ask different questions. Encourage debate and conversation. Have your own voice and always be yourself. Always supply fresh and new content.

Always do little updates to your blog. Move with the times. Check out the competition and see what new design updates they are doing. Think of ways you can improve your site and add or remove things that you think will improve it. You don't need to keep doing redesigns, and your readers might not like it if you do, but little tweaks here and there to improve it are a good idea.

Everything is achievable in life it you just break it down into little pieces. It is less daunting and you will achieve the big goals you have set.

Always make sure your content is unique. This will drive more traffic. Also consider doing YouTube videos.

Hopefully deciding what to write about will be easy for you. It will be the thing you love, the thing you are passionate about, that thing that you are very good at. That thing you never get bored of. That thing could be many things or just a few which you can then put a unique spin on and write about on your blog. Your niche does not have to be a topic, it can be your own unique voice.

Because my blog, http://frostmagazine.com is written in the lifestyle niche I have been able to cover a lot of topics, and also find out what works and what doesn't. This variety has been great when coming up with article ideas but has also given me experience in a number of different niches. Of course it means that not every article suits everyone but it does mean I have reached a wider audience.

Having a niche for your blog can make sure it is successful. You can become an expert in your field and readers know exactly what they are getting. Not everyone wants to do this however, and plenty of people have varied interests. Although you can have a blog for each interest it is time-consuming and harder to maintain more than one blog. Frost Magazine is a thinker's lifestyle magazine. We cover lots of different things but our niche is that we are selling a certain lifestyle. We cover restaurant reviews, wine reviews, food, cooking, travel, writing, book reviews, beauty reviews, news, feminism ... yes a pretty broad scope. It hasn't stopped us building up a loyal readership. Our bounce rate (when a visitor to your site only reads one page and then leaves) is very low and readers tend to read at least three articles before going somewhere else. So don't feel like you need to choose a niche but do be aware that, if you do, it will probably be much easier to build an audience. At least initially.

Another reason why choosing a niche is easier is that people like to put things in categories. A lot of sites will rate blogs in their category: best beauty blogs, best lifestyle, etc. If you are hard to place then that can work against you. I have found this with Frost. Lifestyle is a pretty broad topic and not everyone knows what to do with it. The benefits for me have far outweighed the cons however.

Although Frost does not have an obvious niche it does have a certain style and it is clear what fits and doesn't. So do know that even if you blog on a few different topics, you can still have a clear voice and vision which will build up a loyal readership. Writing from the heart and being genuine also helps build up a loyal readership.

You don't need to target your blog to a niche, you can target it to a certain audience. As an example you could target your blog to people interested in an alternative lifestyle, vegans, the fashion-conscious or people who are environmentally conscious. This would allow you to write about a huge variety of topics but there would still be a niche: the targeted audience. This has worked well for many blogs and could also make for a profitable blog as advertisers scramble to sell to your demographic. Frost's demographic is professional people, mostly women but also a healthy amount of men, with a high disposable income who like to play hard and work hard. They are interested in the best things in life. So target a niche or an audience but no matter what: be unique.

Some blogs are very picture heavy. Their great photography is one of their main selling points. A picture tells a thousand words and human beings are very visual.

The pros of having a blog with a niche are: building a community. People like to feel like they are part of something. People will want to read your posts but also interact with like-minded people. Blogging in one area will also see that blog becoming a trusted source in that niche. It will give the blog credibility. This could even lead to you becoming an expert in your field. You could even become a brand ambassador or sponsored by a company that suits your niche. This is even better if you have a product or service you can sell in this area. You may even find that you become the go-to person in that area and find that people seek you out for your expertise, meaning your customers come to you, cutting out a lot of work.

When your blog is about one subject it is easier for contextual advertising, like Google AdSense to target the advertising on your blog. The adverts will be more relevant to your readers and more likely to make you money. Niche blogs may also be more attractive to advertisers in general as the blog will be relevant to their products and/or services.

A niche blog may also find their SEO (search-engine-optimisation) is better because search engines like sites that have clear topics and pages that are similar in content to each other.

In the film industry actors are told to let themselves be typecast and then diversify. The same can be applied to blogs. After you become known in one field you will have a fan base which can follow you into a similar topic. This may not work if you go from country music to heavy-metal rock but could work for a variety of other topics. From lifestyle to parenting, or incorporating another topic, such as food for example.

If you are selling something specific having a niche blog in that topic can really help with your conversion rate. You are more likely to sell something to people who are interested in the product you are selling.

When choosing your niche make sure it is something you are passionate about and could still write about in years to come. It takes years of work to build a blog and if you are not truly interested in your niche, that will come across to your readers. Choosing something you love and can endlessly write about is the key to choosing a successful niche. You don't have to be an expert in your chosen topic. You can make it clear you are a beginner and build up your readership that way. People will be happy to go on your journey with you.

You could choose a popular niche to blog about, or one that is not as popular but that will have less competition from other blogs on the same subject. There are a significant amount of beauty blogs for example, but not as many on trainspotting. But how many people are interested in trainspotting? That is the question you need to ask about your chosen niche. You don't have to choose a topic based on popularity but if you want to make your blog into a business then make sure the readership is out there. Analyse the market, read other blogs, look at Twitter and Facebook. Go to a newsagent and look at the magazines. Do your research and look at this from a business point of view. Go to Google Trends (www.google.com/trends) and type in some keywords of your chosen niche. You would not launch any other business without knowing there was a market for your product so make sure there are people out there who will read your blog. Watch out for trends and what is popular. Again, you don't need to go for what is most popular but do research the market.

When researching the market it is very important to check out the competition. Whilst you should not look at other bloggers as the competition (see them as friends and supporters, make a community and link to each other's sites instead), research will help you see what works and what doesn't.

- What are they doing right?
- What are they doing wrong?
- How are they marketing themselves?
- What is their niche?
- How do the monetise their content?
- What advertising network are they with?
- What is missing?
- What are they not doing?
- How often do they post?
- How long are their posts?
- Do readers comment?
- What is their design like?

The things to look into when deciding on your niche are: audience size, whether it is financially viable, if you can continue to write blog posts on that subject for years to come and the level of competition.

If you come up with a topic and there is no competition in that area you may be original, or the subject may not be interesting enough for a successful blog. You can test a subject by writing about it as a category on an existing blog to see if people are interested. Or start a free WordPress blog on the subject, taking it more seriously if the blog finds a market. The market your blog finds does not need to be about a hugely popular topic, you can make a decent amount of money with a blog with a smaller niche which has a loyal and dedicated readership than a blog about a more popular topic which has much more competition. You can even find a popular topic but do it in a way that everyone else isn't, making your own sub-niche in a crowded area.

After you have chosen your topic you then need to choose some sub-topics. If you look at other blogs you will see that they have categories, usually in the top bar. These will be different depending on the niche of that blog. A beauty blog for example will have makeup, nails, hair, skin, fragrance etc. Each category may even have more sub-categories in a drop-down menu. So while there is a clear theme, there are also a number of other sub-themes and the readers can also go to these. If a beauty blog started doing DIY projects then it would confuse readers and they would go elsewhere.

Frost Magazine calls itself a thinker's lifestyle magazine. These are the categories in our menu bar: entertainment, life & style, culture, beauty & health, love, news, restaurant & hotel reviews, weddings, the film set, parenting, travel, about us and the Frost Magazine team. This is a lot of categories to have: that's OK. One of the main reasons I called Frost an online magazine is because it covers a lot of different areas of life. BUT we do in a very Frost way. It is clear what fits and what doesn't. As your blog progresses you will know exactly what suits it and what does not. You are building a brand, that brand can branch out into other areas, but it must always retain its unique voice. Your main theme can be broad, but it shouldn't contain everything. The things you write about should fit into one of your themes or sub-themes. Of course, if you want to write about something new you could add a new category. Your readers may love it or hate it. I have done this quite a few times and been pleasantly surprised by the results. Sometimes I added a new category after writing a post which got a lot of hits and positive feedback. Don't be scared to try something new. Even if it doesn't work, you tried. You will be tempted to use the audience you have to get your opinion on a certain topic across sometimes. I say, go for it but don't make a habit out of it. And no ranty posts just because you have had a bad day and want to seek revenge in the way only a writer can. Always think positive unless you can put a good, humorous spin on your rant.

The key is to have a unique blog which adds something to an already crowded market. So whether your blog has a niche or not, make sure it has a voice. Whatever subject you choose, you need to be able to write about it continually. The good thing about Frost Magazine is that there are a variety of subjects it covers, if I get bored of one, I can switch to another. So if you choose to have just one niche make sure you have enough content to write about for years to come, whether through your knowledge or by looking for inspiration elsewhere. You cannot build a successful blog without fresh content so keep that in mind. Google your niche to make sure there will be enough inspiration out there for you to get a constant source of ideas.

Your niche will also affect what advertising options will work for your blog. Check out other blogs in your chosen niche to see how they are monetising their site and what advertising network they are with, if any. Do as much research as you can. Also find out affiliate programs in your chosen area. There probably will be some. Also check out what kind of percentage you get when you sell something via your blog. Some are better than others.

The most important thing is that you love what you write about. My writer friends would still write if they won the lottery. Blogging is hard, tedious and you have to constantly come up with fresh content. No matter how much you love it there will be days, in fact weeks, where you find it hard to motivate yourself and write anything but you must. Writing about something you genuinely love and have an interest in will make those tough days much easier.

Blogging Research Tools

Yahoo have Yahoo Buzz (buzz.yahoo.com/) which lets you know what people are searching for on Yahoo.

To help with your research you can use http://www.wordtracker.com, which is a popular keyword research tool. It has a free trial which is limited but useful. It will let you know how many people are searching for certain things and the number of other sites competing in that niche.

Google Blog Search is useful for finding out who else is blogging on your chosen niche.

Technorati used to list blogs and have a Top 100 blog list but they have stopped. To the dismay of many bloggers.

I have already mentioned Google Trends but Google also have an AdWords Keyword Tool. You will have to sign up to use it but you won't have to pay anything or advertise to use it. It is a very useful tool and will show you how many people are searching for that particular keyword and how many advertisers are competing in that area. It also tells you how many people searched for that keyword in the past month and other keywords that relate to that specific keyword, which is interesting and helpful.

Some niches to consider: finance, money-saving tips, recipes, food, DIY, household tips, parenting,

I know I have written a lot about finding out what readers want and giving it to them but also keep in mind that you must be authentic. People read your blog because they like your perspective and unique take on things. Follow all of the advice about giving the audience what they want but never be put off writing personal pieces or what you want. Even if they get fewer hits than other posts. You have an outlet for your ideas and posts, many writers do not have that, use it to its advantage. Don't lose yourself in a quest for hits.

Don't copy other bloggers, do your own thing. Be authentic and real.

Here are some other ways to draw people in: a compelling argument, write about a personal struggle, challenge people, stories that touch people, tips, advice, DIY projects, amazing recipes with pictures that make your mouth water, unique observations, being funny, getting people talking and sharing, something that makes people feel good about themselves, a good blog design.

Make sure your blog is easy to navigate.

Good grammar and spelling are essential. Everyone makes mistakes but do proof-read your work before you hit publish. Make sure your writers do the same.

High quality pictures are important, even if they are just taken on an iPhone. People will also be more likely to share a post with a picture. They look better on social media too, creating a higher click-through rate.

Tip - Things to avoid:

- Putting up any old article just so there will be new content. Quality is the aim.
- Rambling posts with no point to them
- Boring and insignificant things about your personal life.
- Rants and venting
- Grammar and spelling errors
- Bad pictures
- Plagiarism: never steal other people's content or pictures. It is not just wrong, it is illegal.
- Just posting press releases
- Stealing other people's ideas and not giving them credit. You can share other people's ideas but give your take on them and always give them credit and a link.
- Just posting something to make money, even though it does not suit your site
- Posting too much or too little

Have a clear vision of what your perfect blog is and then take it step-by-step to make it so.

Make a Plan And Set Targets. Always work on building up your following on your social networks.

STAYING MOTIVATED

It can be hard to stay motivated. Especially when you don't see fast results. The difference between those who have a successful blog and those who don't is simply the ability to motivate. Some days will be harder than others but if you keep at it the hard work will pay off. Another great thing is that if you want a day off, you just have to schedule a blog post and off you go. Don't be scared to take a day off. I used to work every day, including weekends and in the end I just got ill. I try not to work weekends anymore and make sure I take some time out every day to recharge. The truth is you must take breaks. If you take breaks you will work better when you come back to the task in hand and will stop yourself burning out. If you need to just write a quick (good!) post and then take the rest of the day off then do so. You don't want to end up hating blogging.

When it comes time to motivate yourself remind yourself that you are building a business. In life you get out what you put in. Even if you spend three hours a day on your blog it can really take off and grow over time. Just remind yourself why you are doing this and give yourself regular breaks.

WORKING FROM HOME: SETTING BOUNDARIES

When you work from home some people won't respect your time and think it is OK to call you, drop by or even ask you to run errands for them. Set your hours and be firm with people. When you sit at your desk you are at work. You may not be in an office but that is irrelevant. If you have to, turn off your phone and politely tell people that you are busy.

Another annoying thing about being self-employed and freelance is that some people will not understand how hard you work, or that it is a real job. Just ignore any jibes and firmly tell people that you work as hard, if not harder, than they do. And just because you can work anywhere that doesn't mean that people can ask you to house-sit for them or that you don't need to be near your own stuff. Also watch out for people expecting to get parcels for them if you live in a house-share. I once lived in a house-share and a few of my housemates very rudely just assumed they could go crazy online shopping and I could spend my day signing for their parcels. Make it clear that although you are at home you are at work.

Chapter 2: Revenue Streams. The Different Options And How To Make Money

When it comes to earning money from blogging the sky is the limit. Pete Cashmore started Mashable in his bedroom in Aberdeen after a bout of ill health. Now he is constantly on lists of the next billionaires and his earnings are in the six figures per month. Michael Arrington sold TechCrunch for $30 million. The potential is limitless. With that in mind here are the ways to make money blogging. Always remember: diversifying income streams reduces risk.

The good thing about a blog is that it costs almost nothing to start up. This makes it unique among other businesses. The startup costs are low so that pretty much anyone can start a blog. This is also probably why there are so many out there. There is one investment that you have to make a lot of however: your time. It is a big one but if you don't put the time in you will never have a successful blog. This chapter is about revenue streams. It may be tempting to try to monetise your blog straight away but don't. Not only will you put any potential readers off but you won't have anything to sell. Work on building up your blog with great content. Many bloggers blog for years before making a profit. You have to have something to monetise before you just put a lot of advertising in.. By all means add some Google AdSense if you really want to but only have subtle advertising in the beginning; you need to build something first. If you just get obsessed with advertising instead of building a great blog then you won't build a great site because you will just put people off.

Don't include a lot of obnoxious advertisements or anything that will put your readers off. Traffic is what you need, not to make a quick buck that will put people off in the long term. You can't make money from a brand that does not exist.

Building your brand and creating great content is the most important thing unless you have hundreds of thousands of page views every month, then focus on monetising.

Although it is not a good idea to get obsessed with advertising too early, it is a good idea to have some on your site just so readers get used to it and then don't get upset when they see ads on the site later.

Focus on your content and promote it well.

Even when you do monetise, it is easy to get despondent sometimes. It takes years to build a blog into a successful business. The thing to remember is that your income will come from multiple sources and all of those smaller payments really do add up. Another thing to remember is that your blog is a business so invest in it. Put some of the advertising money aside and put it back into your blog. Put it into the design or marketing. Sign up for a conference like the one Mumsnet does. You will meet brands and other bloggers.

Blogging is not a get-rich scheme, nor is it easy money, but it is possible to make a living from blogging. Steadily grow your blog and it will pay off in the end.

When you start a blog you will get a lot of emails from companies and advertising/marketing companies. Do not take every advertising opportunity you are offered. Only work with companies that you believe in. Always keep your integrity. Always serve your readers above all else.

Work on your blog every day. It is your business so invest in it. Work on it in the evenings until you can afford to quit your day job. Work it around your life but put in the time. It takes hard work and sacrifice to be successful in any business, blogging is no exception. Build an audience first. Don't rush to the finishing line.

UDEMY.

Udemy is an online marketplace for video courses. You can do a course on any topic and then publish it. The course can be paid or free and Udemy has over two million students. Create a course that is relevant to your blog and mention your blog in the lectures and include the URL in the notes too. Udemy also allows you to send emails to your students. Don't spam them, send them relevant posts instead and only things you think they will be interested in.

Video courses. You can also use a product called Fedora to host and sell video courses. Produce a video course on the niche that your blog covers. You can create an online school without any technical or design experience. It is easy to use. They have a basic plan which has no upfront costs.

Paid Content or Products.

You can write a book on the niche your blog covers. You might even find that you have enough good material to make the process less painful on your blog already. Use Gumroad to put it behind a paywall (which means visitors will have to pay to access it). Having premium content on your site is one way to make money but you will need loyal readers.

For your book, search for the topic of it and then use the words and phrases in the title, subtitle and Amazon description using Google Keyword Planner so your title stands out and is easy to find.

Consulting and coaching. If you are qualified in your niche you could do consulting or coaching. Either for a one-off fee or on a monthly retainer.

Another way to make money from premium content is to have content that is only available to paying subscribers. This can be done behind a paywall or in a newsletter.

Try the different revenue streams to see which ones work for you. Drop the ones that don't work. You will be surprised how a few different revenue streams can add up.

Every blogger will earn a living in a slightly different way. There is no 'set' way to do it. What works for your site won't work for someone else. Seek out opportunities that are right for you and don't compare yourself to anyone else. Take it slowly.

Think about your blog genre when it comes to the best method of monetising.

You can show some advertisements from friends or local businesses for free to encourage other people to advertise and show that you are open for business. You can also put AdSense on your blog immediately.

Some readers are put off by a blog with lots of advertisement and I don't blame them. Some of it is very distracting. Especially if it redirects you to a different page before bringing you back to that page, or floats around. However, readers should not be annoyed by some AdSense or banner advertisement. If they do then it is their problem. Sorry to be harsh but very few things in life are free and a lot of work goes into a successful blog, if they begrudge you making a little bit of money for your effort then see it as their problem, not yours.

Always add up whether the advertising is worth it. If it brings the tone of your blog down, it is not and if you only earn a little from it and your blog looks better without it then just turn it off and find another source of advertising revenue. Looking professional is always better than earning a few bucks.

Try to make your advertising look good.

Here are some advertising options you can go with.

Ad Networks

Google AdSense (the largest and most common. There can only be three Google ads displayed on your site at any given time.)

Google AdSense is a program from Google which matches the advertisements on your blog to your blog content. This makes the adverts relevant and your viewers more likely to click on them. Google AdSense is very easy to use; you basically just copy and paste the code onto your site. You don't have to do any work after the code is there. Just go to google.com/adsense and answer the questions. Revenue will be based on how many people come to your site and click through so the higher your traffic, the more money you will make.

There are a number of advertising networks out there specifically for blogs. They will take a percentage which varies depending on which network you go with. You can choose the size of the advertisements.

- Lijit
- Pulse Point
- BlogHer
- Burst
- media.net (Yahoo! ads)

Ad networks work with a large number of advertisers who then pay that network to place their ad on the blogs in that network. You will be paid per click or per thousand views (CPM)

Many of the below are American.

- Handpicked Collective (a marketing agency with hundreds of blogs in its network. I am with Hand-picked and have been for years. They do banner advertising and also sponsored posts. They are a good company which is run by friendly people who really know their stuff. Highly recommended. You need at least 10,000 unique users a month to join).

- Skimlinks (I use Skimlinks on Frost. They are easy to use and very good to deal with. I can highly recommend them. They provide in-text advertising. Their brilliant software automatically turns certain URLs into clickable affiliate links, providing they are an affiliate with Skimlinks)

- Chitika (they use reader's search queries and provide targeted ads)

- Price grabber (CPM-based)

- Rivit Media (For DIY and crafting blogs.)

- Pulse Point (lets bloggers set their own rates)

- Federated Media (Lets ad buyers buy ads on specific blogs, focuses on independent bloggers who have a loyal following.)

- AdGenta

- Martha's Circle (Martha Stewart's blog network. Includes and advertising network. They focus on food and DIY.

- RadiumOne (multimedia ad network. They offer options for mobile advertising and social sharing advertisement).

- Blogads (They allow blogger to sell their own ad space and set their own prices. Also lets you accept or reject certain ads.)

- DoubleClick

- Vibrant (contextual in-text ads. CPM based).

- Kontera (Contextual in-text advertising. They also offer the option to syndicate your content)

- Lifetime Moms (for moms obviously. Smaller ad network)

- GlamMedia (large ad network which focuses on women and lifestyle. US and UK.)

- Kanoodle

- Lanista Concepts (Provides competitive CPM rates)

- EverythingMom Network (Canadian. For mom and family bloggers)

- MTV Ad networks (music and entertainment)

- Moms Media (has advanced targeting options)

- Text Link Ads

- IntelliTXT

- Technorati Media (ad network for bloggers. Huge scale. They are a known name and do a wide variety of topics)

- YPN

- Adversal (requires at least 50,000 page views every month)

- Beacon Ads (lets bloggers charge for their own ads and set their own prices. Is a religious ad network)

- Burst Media (Do specific targeted ads. They have Burst Mom for mummy bloggers, Burst Stadium for sport and Burst Ella for fashion and design)

- Tribal Fusion (One of the largest ad networks. They will only accept bloggers with over half a million visitors every month).

- Cox Digital Solutions. (is a network of networks. Has over two hundred niche advertising networks.

- Sovrn (used to be Lijit) Associated with Federation Media. Large with a good variety of CPM ads.

- Linkshare. Receive a cheque as soon as earnings reach £25

- BlogHer Publishing Network (American)

Phew. That is quite a lot of choice. It would be impossible to go with all of these networks, and some want you to sign to them exclusively. The best way to choose one is to do your homework. Research each one, look at the blogs who use them. There may be a lot of trial and error but you will find the right ad network for you.

Marketing Agencies

Frost is with Handpicked Media. Handpicked do the advertising for Frost and take a percentage. The adverts are relevant to the content on Frost. There are other marketing agencies similar to Handpicked like Glam Media, which a few of my friends are with.

Placement

It is very easy to get excited about monetising your blog and obsessing over what works and what doesn't, doing lots of different tweaks. The truth is, if you get fewer than 50,000 page views a month then you should instead focus on building traffic and creating amazing content instead. Sure, sign up to Google AdSense and get some banner ads on. You can sign up to a few blog networks too but then leave it. Revisit your advertising strategy when your traffic is higher, before that, you are wasting your time. Focus on the content and building traffic first.

According to Google, the best place to put ads on your blog is directly above, below or to the left of your main blog content. This makes sense of course; we read from left to right and look from top to bottom. This is human nature so use it for your advertising strategy. Doing this will make your advertising more noticeable and readers more likely to click on it. This only matters for pay-per-click (PPC) advertising. CPM advertising will get the same impression no matter where they are based generally, although if they are placed at the bottom and your readers don't scroll all the way down then they will get fewer impressions. Don't worry too much about this, most CPM ads will take this into account.

So, keeping this in mind, one of the things you can do to optimise your ad revenue is to move your sidebar to the left-hand side. It might seem like a huge task, and it will certainly be annoying and require a lot of work, but it could make a difference. Your regular readers should adapt to the change. You don't need to do this, and it might not make a huge difference, but it might work for you and be worth the effort.

The best thing to do with ads is to make them work with your site and the design of it. They should look natural. Make sure your site layout highlights your amazing content, not the ads. It is important that ads do not overwhelm readers.

Make sure the higher-paying ads are in the most prominent position. Give premium placement according to how profitable they are. This is called 'waterfalling'.

You can optimise your ad placement using an ad-serving service. Google do one called Google DoubleClick For Publishers (DFP). DFP is an ad server that allows you to serve all of your ad tags at the same time. I have never used it myself but I have heard it is time-consuming and quite complicated to set up. DFP is a free service. You can add all of your various network codes and CPMs of each of your networks and DFP then automatically serves the highest paying ad. It even makes Google's own AdSense compete with all of the other networks and makes the ads run more efficiently and load at the same time. You will need to take the time to learn how to work DFP as it requires some programming and coding. If that all sounds a bit much you could hire a DFP expert to set it up for you, maintain it and monitor it.

Test each ad to see how it performs. Give them at least two weeks to see how they perform. Keep a record of the results and remember to update it. Only keep ads that earn the highest CPM.

AdThrive DFP experts: http://www.adthrive.com/. I have never used them myself but have heard good things.

SOME MORE OPTIMISATION TIPS FOR YOUR ADS.

Apply to lots of ad networks and compare their CPMs. In fact, apply to every single one and then see what your options are. Make sure they are the best ones; check out their reputations and the other blogs in their networks. Apply to as many as possible and then see which ones work for you.

Place as many above the fold as you can. At least one of your ads should be above the fold. More if you can.

When it comes to ad networks, look at their CPM carefully. Also check for fill rate which is the percentage of ads that get shown per page view. Make sure nothing is inflated.

Google AdSense and Yahoo ads only sell their own ads and these are then put on their own blog publisher's sites. Other ad networks will sell some of their own ads and then syndicate the rest. This is why sometimes you see the same ad on many different sites. Google AdSense works on a pay-per-click (PPC) basis. Some ad networks will specify an above-the-fold placement ad. Above the fold is a term that comes from the print publishing industry. It means, with thanks to Wikipedia, "Above the fold is the upper half of the front page of a newspaper where an important news story or photograph is often located." So it means at the top of your site before readers have to scroll down. It is basically the most prominent place on your blog.

CONTENT ADVERTISING AND SEO

The people who come to your site via Google are more likely to click on Google ads. This is obvious of course. The user searches for something specific, shoes, for example, they end up on your site with the targeted Google ads, they read the article they found via Google, see the ad and end up clicking on it. This is not an accident and is the way Google works. The important thing to remember when you are online is that if you are not paying: you're the product. Never is this truer than with Google.

Check your search terms. Monitor your search engine traffic terms with Google Analytics to see which give the most traffic. This is what people will buy from you. Tweak your advertising and affiliates accordingly. To see your traffic terms in Google Analytics go to standard report- traffic sources- search- organic. You will then be able to see a list of search terms that visitors used to get to your blog. Since Google now allows users to cloak their search terms the first thing on the list might be 'not provided'. Try to find out which search term links to which specific post or page. The easiest way to do this might be to take the search term and Google it yourself. Once you have found out which post people are going to, optimise that specific post/page with a targeted ad from one of your ad networks, you could even do this within the actual text post. Clever, right? This just goes to show that when it comes to running a blog as a business you need imagination and to be able to think outside of the box. Treat it like a business and it will become one. Highly targeted ads on the right post can bring in good money, I have a few posts with affiliate links in that tend to make a little bit of money on an ongoing basis. Even if it is a few pounds here and there, you will be surprised how much it starts to build up. Use an ad network that allows you to customise ads for these highly targeted posts. media.net is good for doing this. media.net use Bing and Yahoo for their ads. They do text ads which you can customise to your site, they don't do image ads.

Make sure the highly targeted banner ads placed within the text have a colour and the content of the ad meld seamlessly with the rest of the site. People do not like obvious advertising and will be less likely to read the post, click on any links and come back to your blog if the advertising is overwhelming or garish. Do this page optimisation for your most popular pages anyway, but especially the posts where the traffic comes from search engines.

If you don't already have Google Analytics then definitely get it immediately. A word of warning though, it can get very addictive. You should spend a good amount of time on Google Analytics doing market research for your blog. It provides a lot of essential information that you can then implement and use to grow your blog and target your audience.

Optimise every single blog post and page and all of your older posts too. It is helpful if you have a niche for targeted ads, it is more likely that people will click on the advertising.

Google AdSense is the biggest and most common ad network. It is high-paying for most bloggers. Watch the Google 'Adsense installation video' if you need any help installing adsense.

Ad networks generally do banner ads (which run at the top or the bottom of your blog and are rectangular. Check out http://frostmagazine.com for reference) and sidebars (which go, yes, in the sidebar. They are smaller, usually square and can run to the left or the right) ads. Sometimes they will do different sizes but these are the industry standard.

Ad Networks are easy to use and can make you a little bit of money, you just install the ads, the readers view or click on the ad and then you make some money. The thing is, these work well if you get a lot of traffic, not so much if you don't. It is not that you will make no money; it just won't be enough to live on. But advertising through ad networks is great because the ads are just there earning you money and you can focus on what is important: creating good content. The good thing about this is that creating good content will get you more traffic which will make you more money. They are a great passive income stream.

Most successful bloggers do not make the bulk of their income from ad networks however. Another problem is that it won't be consistent. Sometimes you make a lot of money from ad networks, other times barely anything. It depends on a number of factors: your readers, their interests, the advertiser. Some of it is like having to be in the right place at the right time. This is another reason why it is good to diversify your traffic. If your blog is in a niche that becomes popular, crafting for example, then advertisers will competitively bid on ad space in that niche. If you are a crafter you will be quids in. The only problem is if your niche falls out of fashion, and it probably will eventually. The advertisers and readers will then go elsewhere, on to the next big thing. Never rely on just one advertising stream.

Optimise ad placement on your blog, add additional ad networks. Diversification is key; make sure no one advertising stream is your only source of income. Not all ad networks just do banner advertisement, they also do social media sharing, RSS feeds, text ads, email and much more.

DIFFERENT TYPES OF AD PAYMENT.

1. CPC which stands for "cost per click". You only get paid when a reader clicks on the advert. Not a fan of these as the advert is still seen by the reader. Which is worth something, surely? CPA stands for "cost per acquisition". You will get paid a commission if a sale or signup is made.

2. CPA stands for "cost per acquisition". You will get paid a commission if a sale or sign up is made.

3. CPM which means "cost per thousand" views. You will be paid a certain amount for how many times the advertisement is viewed. Each view is referred to as an "impression". M is the Roman numeral for 1000.

SELLING ADVERTISING YOURSELF.

Whilst it can be easy to just go with a marketing agency or an advertisement system, you might earn more, and have more control if you do your own advertising. You might not want the hassle or want to put in the time and effort. In which case, giving a percentage to someone else is a perfect compromise. If you do want to do your own advertising however then you will need a couple of things. Starting with...

SELL YOUR NICHE.

If your blog has a niche and a targeted audience then you can use this to your benefit. If the advertisers buy advertisement space with a mainstream site or publication then they may reach lots of people, but you can reach the people who will actually buy their products and be interested in their brand. Don't pretend that you have a higher readership than you have, but do point out that you can do highly targeted advertising to the exact people who will be interested in their brand.

WHO TO SELL TO?

Which advertisers should you target? A good place to start is looking at which brands are advertising on competitors' sites. Contact them with a brief email, telling them about your blog and include all of your advertising statistics and rates. Ask them if they would like to advertise on your blog too. The good thing about this is that these companies which already advertise on blogs will be open to it, not all companies are forward looking and realise how popular blogs are yet. They will learn though. If you have Google AdSense on your blog at the moment then you can take a look at which brands are advertising on your blog and then contact them directly and do a deal with them.

Selling advertising is a numbers game and the more companies you contact the more likely you are to find an advertiser for your blog. Make a list of brands and companies that suit your audience and then start contacting them one-by-one. You will learn a lot and get there in the end.

To make things easier create a general letter that you can copy and paste. Then tweak this for each advertiser. Include the following information on your general letter: Start with an introduction, keep it brief and then say why you are contacting them. Tell them what they have to gain and give brief details about your blog such as readership demographic, topics you cover, stats like uniques, page views and subscribers. Finish with your different advertising options, what kind of advertising you can provide and the price.

Keep all of this brief and do not overdo it. People don't have the time to read a long essay and it would also look unprofessional. Just include the bullet points and then if they are interested you can give them more information when they reply to you. Keep the general letter at two or three paragraphs maximum.

Keep looking at other blogs and sites which target the topics you cover and see who is advertising on these sites and also look at their advertising pages and see what they are saying and what they are charging. Always keep an eye on the competition and do market research in your industry.

It is a very good idea to have a PayPal account. Although PayPal takes a fee (an oversized one in my opinion) a lot of advertisers will prefer to pay you this way as it is easier than a bank transfer. It also makes payments easier as all you have to do is give your email address to the advertisers and then they can send you money. Sign up at http://paypal.co.uk

You can also give them your bank details or send an invoice. No matter what payment option you choose, make sure that advertisers can pay easily. The easier you make things for people the more likely they will keep returning and give you more business.

Keep your advertising at a competitive rate to begin with. The internet and blogging industry is hugely over-populated so you have to offer advertisers something that no one else does, or at least value for money. The advertisers will want a return on their investment; do everything you can to make sure your advertisers get value for money.

As a start you could charge $0.50 CPM which would be 50 cents per 1000 views. This would mean that your blog would earn $50 month if it got 100,000 hits. (Most ad networks and agencies are American so you will be paid in dollars a lot. This obviously means less money if you are UK based because of the exchange rate).

Be flexible with your terms and even offer free trials. If you are unsure on what to charge and you use Google AdSense then analyse how much money you would have made through AdSense, then adjust your rates accordingly. Sell your advertisement on a monthly basis so people don't feel locked in. Offer a discount for long-term deals

You can sell adverting in different formats. These include banner and sidebar options. The banners can be either headers or footers. Most blogs offer the small and square 125-by-125 pixel ad option. These are not only popular but tend to fit well into sidebars. These are also good because you could easily fit up to four on your blog and it won't look overdone. Some advertisers will want a different size. If they want a larger one then charge them more, as you could have sold the space to a different advertiser.

Don't overcrowd your blog with adverts. This not only puts off readers but it also puts off advertisers. It will make your blog look unprofessional and over-crowded. The content should be king and the main focus, nothing else. A banner ad on the top and maximum of four in the sidebar should be the total. Don't just look like you are money hungry and don't care about the reader experience. This will put people off.

Make sure the advertisements on your blog suit it and look good.

AN ADVERTISEMENT PAGE

You have to let advertisers know that they can advertise on your blog and have all of the information they will need available to them. Make sure that it is clear how to contact you. You can have your advertising rates on your site or just somewhere handy where you can send them along. I would keep mine private but that is your decision. Make sure it is clear what the advertiser is getting from your blog and what you have to offer them. Let them know what your blog is about and that you are worth it. Make it clear why someone would purchase an advertisement on your blog.

You can initially give some free advertisement for a limited time on the basis that they give you feedback on clicks, sales and any other comments. They may even decide to advertise for real after the free trial. This may also inspire other companies to advertise with you, if they see the competition advertising with you.

You can put 'advertise here' banners on your blog.

MEDIA PACK

You can also put a media pack together. Print magazines do this and so do many blogs and sites. The information in your media pack would include your blog stats: readership, uniques, hits, demographics like age and gender and then your rates for different type of advertisement that you feature on your blog. Show that you know your audience well. If you want, you can pay ComScore or Quantcast to get more detailed stats. You could also say what keyword and phrases you rank for in Google. Stats, rates, reader demographics, advertisement options. Make this document look as professional as possible. Remember to include your current contact details and update all of the relevant details as they change. If you can, include testimonials and references from past advertisers.

Create a media and advertising kit. Here is what your advertising kit should include: blog description, traffic statistics, reader demographic, advertising opportunities available, pricing info, picture or logo, biography or about, contact information and testimonials/any references. Include any awards you or the magazine has won and any qualifications or other accomplishments. Also include any media experience like interviews and press cuttings.

In your traffic statistics include your monthly page views, unique visitors, email subscribers, social media followers of Facebook, Twitter, Google +, YouTube, Pinterest, Instagram and your Google page rank and Alexa ranking. Doing a PDF is a good idea.

Setting up an email specifically for advertising enquires is a good idea.

Make sure your media kit is easy to read. Make sure it is formatted well. Use bullet points, headings and sub-headings. Don't include too much information and make sure that any dense text is broken up with spaces, pictures or boxes,

Send your media kit to advertisers who request it but you could also do a version of your media kit as a page on your site. Don't include any information you don't want made public, like your ad rates. This should hopefully draw in other advertisers and they can ask for the full media kit if they are interested.

KEEP YOUR BLOG PROFESSIONAL.

Always keep in mind that your blog should be professional. The wrong kind of content will put buyers off and bring down your brand. Being negative or swearing a lot will put advertisers off. As will criticising certain brands and products unnecessarily. This doesn't mean you should not give honest reviews, just make sure they are fair and balanced. Never lie, your loyalty is to your readers but don't outright attack brands unless they truly deserve it. Make sure you don't scare any advertisers with unprofessional behaviour.

Analyse your readers' demographics and then think about what companies want to reach those demographics. This means you have something to sell and have a USP (unique selling point).

Tip - Advertising options: guest-blogging, consultations, public speaking engagements, affiliates, sponsored posts, teaching, videos and working with brands and being an ambassador.

SELLING YOUR OWN PRODUCTS.

One of the best things about blogs is that they give you a platform. You can then sell your products to your growing fan base. The product will have to be within the niche of your blog but the possibilities are endless. If you blog about jewellery, you can sell that. You can write e-books about whatever you are an expert in. Find the gap and create a product to fill it. I wrote my book How To Be A Successful Actor: Becoming an Actorpreneur because people kept asking me how they could become an actor, or be a successful one. Make money from your knowledge and talent. Listen to people and what they want. What do your readers want? What is popular on your blog? Find out what your readers want and give it to them and then create products that fill the need.

CLASSES AND TEACHING.

Do workshops or online classes. You can do this as a video, PDF or in person. If you do them in person then just hire a local venue. This is also a good way to build word-of-mouth. You can do classes on anything you have an expertise in. You could even do them through Google hangouts.

You could include a link to your Etsy shop or another online shop. Handmade products can sell very well.

You could also offer services like writing, proofreading, programming, consulting, organising, web design, decorating, photography, catering, baking ... the list is endless. It all depends on your blog niche. The wonderful thing about having a blog is that you write about a certain area and people want to read it, it gives you the voice and authority to then sell that service professionally. Just make sure you can do the job efficiently.

The opportunities for making money with a blog are endless. All you need is imagination.

PRIVATE ADVERTISING.

Private advertising is when an advert or link on your site is paid directly by the advertiser to you and not via an ad network. You can use a marketing person, a sales person, a service or sell private advertising yourself. You can handle ad sales yourself.

Doing private advertising yourself is scary and can be overwhelming. The more you do it, the easier it will get. Keep at it.

Only use opportunities that suit your core values and fit your brand.

BRAND RELATIONSHIPS.

CREATING YOUR OWN BRAND STRATEGY.

Have clear-cut guidelines. Make your own rules. You can have private sidebar advertising, review products, incorporate content advertising, become a spokesperson for a specific brand or product. You could do YouTube videos featuring the product or underwritten posts, where a brand chooses a topic and you get a comment and introduction at the bottom. Think of different ways you can offer brands to promote them and their products.

You could also offer a month or week long sponsorship to one company for that time. This could include an introduction, a sidebar banner advert and a post written about the company.

You can manage sidebar ads throughout services like passionfruitads.com or adproval.com These both allow advertisers to sign up to their services, upload their ads and then you give the final approval. Limiting the quantity creates more demand.

Set your ad rates. Charge what the market will allow. If you are getting a lot of interest, you might not be charging enough. On the other hand, if you are too expensive, then you probably won't get any so might need to lower your price or get more traffic.

Be secure in your blog and what it is worth. Approach advertisers with confidence. Know what your brand is about so you can sell it well. You should be able to accurately describe your brand in 30 seconds.

You could put an ad in your newsletter or e-edition of your magazine, especially if you have lots of subscribers. Have a clearly defined policy of what you will and will not do.

WHERE TO FIND POTENTIAL ADVERTISERS

You can use social media agencies like Yoked, Social Spark, Pollinate and Clever Girls. They offer campaigns which you apply for.

Blog conferences: great for networking. The sponsors of the conference itself, and brands there will be open to advertising with bloggers. Some brands still see blogs as an unknown quantity so they don't know how to work with bloggers. Check the sponsor list before you go to the blog conference and make a note of the ones you want to work with and think would work with your blog. You can even make a note of some advertising ideas and pitching for specific sponsors. Print your media kit out and include some extra information on how you would work with that brand and then connect with the main person from that brand. Take some time and be passionate and professional.

You will find that you start getting a lot of PR press releases as time goes on. Most of the emails you get from PR people will be rubbish. Sometimes you will get an email from a brand or a PR company that you actually want to work with. If so then use the contact to your advantage. Send a polite, professional email, along with your media kit stating what you could offer them. If you have an advertising idea then you can also share that with them.

CONTACTING BRANDS UNSOLICITED

If you really love a brand then don't be scared to get in touch with them. The worst that can happen is that they say no, and that is not that big a deal. Send an unsolicited pitch to the brand. A professional and polite email introducing yourself and your brand is key. Include your advertising proposal and any ideas. Keep the email brief and only go into more detail if the company responds. Include something that will draw the brand in, like a high readership.

When it comes to advertising always be honest with your readers and brand. Don't promote something you don't believe in. Always be polite and professional. Dress well and always proof-read emails and posts. Manners cost nothing. Be clear with the brand about what is offered and not. This will stop confusion or problems later on. Get everything in writing and do not sign anything until you have read it thoroughly.

Developing relationships with brands will probably take time, weigh up if you think it is worth it for you and your brand. Once you have established contact with a brand, always do what you can to maintain it.

Send press releases to the media. Talk to PR agencies and manufacturers.

PRs, journalists and writers search the web looking for good sites. If yours is of a high standard then they will be interested. Write newsworthy stories and be original.

WORKING WITH BRANDS

Many bloggers work with brands. Some even have their own make up or clothing range. Bip Ling even became a model for clothing brand Fashion 21.

Never promote a brands campaign unless they are paying you. I once saw an advert for a certain brand everywhere. The PR company got in touch with me and asked me to feature it, I asked them their fee and they said they didn't have any money. What they actually meant was that they did not respect bloggers enough to pay them and just expected them to feature the video and campaign for free. So not okay. Brands like new bloggers because they tend to do things for free. Don't undervalue yourself. Remember that the PR person is paid to do their job, your time is worth more than some free stuff that they get for cost. They want free publicity. Remember how much your time is worth and only do things you get something out of.

Tip

- *Make a list of brands and businesses that operate in your niche. Call their head office.*
- *Stick at it, people will find you. PR and media will find you too.*
- *Build up your social media following too as advertisers will take this into consideration.*

SPONSORED POSTS, ADVERTORIALS AND BRAND PROMOTION

A sponsored post is when a company pays you to write a post. I used to earn a lot of money from these until Google decided to penalise people who paid for links. Of course people still requested to 'guest post'. They just used the new Google rules as an excuse to not pay anymore. In saying that, you can still earn money doing sponsored posts; just include a no-follow link code at the beginning and end of the code. Make sure you clearly state that it is a sponsored post. It is not a legal requirement in the UK but is best practice. Advertorial comes from a mash up of advert and editorial. It is basically the same thing as a sponsored post although the brand will probably write it and you just feature it. All of the big print magazines do these.

This is how to do a nofollow link: <a rel="nofollow" href=http://www.frostmagazine.com/>sponsoredpost</a> You would include your own URL and anchor text.

Initially you can make between £50-100 for a sponsored post and then re-evaluate your fee later.

Advertorials: ebuzzing.com and payperpost.com

You can use social media agencies like Yoked, Social Spark, Pollinate and Clever Girls. They offer campaigns which you apply for.

You will be paid for writing about a product. You can write whatever you want and tailor it to your blog.

This means working directly with the brand to promote them or one of their products. A sponsored post is either written by you or the company. You will probably get sponsored posts via a media/ brand agency or your blog network if you are with one.

A sponsored post is usually you writing about a certain topic chosen by the brand and including a link to their brand. Sponsored posts should have 'Sponsored Post' written at the bottom of the page. A lot of the time sponsored posts are product reviews. Be choosy when it comes to product review sponsored posts: only take on products you believe in. Always make sure your sponsored content is engaging and well-written, not just an advertisement.

Find out your readers' interests and what they are willing to spend money on. This will take trial and error but occasionally some things will tank and others will take off. You never know but you can improve your success rate.

Other brand promotion/sponsored posts: paid product giveaways, conference sponsorship, social media promotion, giveaways, brand ambassadorship. These can also mean long-running posts.

Don't waste your time reviewing small products and doing small competitions just to get some free stuff. This will take your mind off the long term goal, deplete your energy and hurt your credibility in the long run. I used to be too polite and agree to review things all the time, and also reviewed everything we got sent. This took up too much of my time and also devalued my blog in the short term. Know your worth and also how much your time is worth. Blogs are very time-consuming, always spend your time in the best way you can. Your time is your investment, don't undervalue it and use it wisely. I still do some reviews but got sick of writing in exchange for free product. It is exhausting and time can be spent growing the blog or taking some time off instead.

FREELANCE BLOGGING

Another great way to make money. Many businesses have their own blogs and if they spot you they could hire you for your writing skills. You could earn a good amount of money blogging for businesses and writing for other blogs too. As you build a following people will be more likely to hire you in the hope that you bring your audience with you. Freelance blogging also allows you to raise your profile and your own blog will probably get more hits as a result.

Let people know you are for hire. Do some free guest blogging to build up a portfolio. Create a banner advert which leads to a page that shows off your freelance writing and says that you are available to hire. Keep it simple. Let people know you are available. Ask around. See if anyone needs any writing done. People might remember you are looking for work and recommend you to people.

Contact businesses. Contact businesses and offer your services. Approach businesses that have just started or have a blog that is not that great and offer your services. The worst that can happen is that they say no. Expect to earn £100 per article to begin with and then increase your price as you go along. You could also offer discounts for businesses that hire you to do a lot of writing.

Keeping a regularly updated blog is great training.

DEVELOP YOUR VOICE - NEWSPAPERS AND MAGAZINES

Think of your blog as your personal CV. It shows you can write well, have an audience and know a lot about a certain subject. Approach publications with article suggestions.

Pitch a short article and then a longer one if that is accepted. You could suggest that you do a series. Always have your copy in on time and be professional. Always share your articles to get more traffic to them and publicise the fact you are in a magazine or newspaper. Write a post about the article you did on your blog.

Do a great pitch; keep it well-structured, short and snappy. Have a good idea. Make sure your idea fits into one of the publications sections. Magazines and newspapers all have different sections i.e.; news, travel, beauty, parenting etc.

You should do a three paragraph pitch. Communicate your idea well. Keep it short. Don't make it too long and complicated. Editors will get hundreds of pitches a week. Have a short heading in bold capitals. Make paragraph one all about the idea. Explain it well. Include facts and other relevant information. Paragraph two could be how the article will be written and who you could contact for quotes. Paragraph three should suggest which section the magazine should go in and how it is relevant to that publication. Help the editor visualise this article in their magazine. Copy and paste the entire thing into the email. Don't add any attachments, this is a pet hate of mine when people send me pitches. I don't have time to download attachments and clicking on them is less convenient than the entire thing being coped into the email body... Make everything as easy for the editor as possible. After you have pitched to an editor, do not pitch to them for at least two weeks. You don't want to come across as desperate.

Email is better than phoning. Always find out the editor's name and contact them directly. If you have any connection to the editor, use it. You may have gone to the same university or have a mutual friend.

If you are offered a payment that you think is too low, don't be scared to reject it or ask for more money. Know your worth. Most editors will try to push a low price onto you. Don't accept the first offer if you think it is too low. Barter a bit.

If you get rejected then try again and ask for feedback on your ideas. Take any comments and modify your approach.

Expect between £200-500 for a short article and £600-800 for an exclusive or a longer articles

LINK BASED ADVERTISING

I use Skimlinks for Frost and I have been impressed. I once wrote an article about engagement rings and someone clicked through and bought a piece of jewellery after reading it. I made a good amount of money and was very pleased indeed. That is the thing about posts and articles: you never know what will take off and what will be a hit, but when something does take off it is very exciting. Even more so when there is a money-making opportunity there and you can actually be paid for some of your hard work.

SELLING PRODUCTS

The products you sell can be your own or someone else's. You can sell e-books, e-courses, things you make like jewellery, blog promotional items, merchandise, anything you can think of. As long as it is good quality and has value. You can also sell services like classes, consulting, party planning, virtual assistant work, social media consulting, speaking or writing.

You can create a page to sell your products. Give a call to action. Create a good sales page.

Places you can sell digital goods. Pretty much all of the below offer a free trial so sign up to various ones and see which one works for you.

- tinypay.me. Is free.
- digitaldeliveryapp.com This one starts at $9 a month. However, they don't charge if you don't sell anything. Is also comprehensive.
- getpd.com Digital Product Delivery starts at $5 per month. I have never used it personally but it has its own WordPress plugin and accepts payment from PayPal, Google checkout, Alertpay and 2checkout. Offers a complete digital good solution.

- pulleyapp.com Costs $6 per month. Lets you put an embeddable 'Buy now' button anywhere.

- e-junkie.com starts at $5 per month. Comprehensive and accepts all major payment services.

SPEAKING ENGAGEMENTS

PUBLIC APPEARANCES

Some bloggers also get paid to attend events. Brands figure that you will write about it afterwards, get them publicity and your readers will also attend. If you are a fashion blogger they may even ask you to host or appear in a fashion show. The possibilities are endless.

Some blogs are launched to build the brand of a specific person. Many publishers now won't even look twice at an author unless they already have an online fan base. A blog can launch your speaking career.

PUBLIC SPEAKING

Do public speaking at seminars, conferences, team building days and industry get-togethers in your niche. You can even do public speaking on cruise ships.

Public speaking agencies: When you are a media personality you can sign up to an agency. Try one of the following: Celeb Agents celebagents.co.uk, Cassius Management Cassiusmanagement.com, and JLA jla.co.uk.

Make sure you highlight your credible qualifications and let people know what you have to offer. Have an interesting story to tell.

Get more work by checking out what events other bloggers speak at and contact the event organiser and make them aware of your presence. Give them your details for future reference.

DOING TALKS

You can be hired to talk at conferences, writers' workshops, in schools and at seminars. I did a talk on acting at a careers day in a school, at the Underwire Film Festival and was also invited to do a talk at Margaret Graham's literary festival in High Wycombe, LitFest. You will not always be paid but even if you are not it is great exposure to promote yourself, your blog and sell any books you have written. Some speaking engagements pay a good amount of money but don't be put off doing some for free. They will be good experience and you can build up your skills and your CV.

Think about your talents and skills. What services can you offer? Can you program? Are you an SEO expert? Can you design well? Illustrate? Cook? Craft? We all have marketable skills, find yours, hone them and then sell them via your blog and guest posts on other peoples' blogs too.

Your blog can also be a great showcase for you. Many people have been plucked from obscurity by writing a blog and now have great careers after showing they have expertise in their field and a sizeable audience. Showing initiative is great in business. On the flipside, people have also lost their jobs from blogging, so if you have a good, well paid job that you love, be careful about what you blog about as you could lose it, even if you blog anonymously.

You could also hire an ad salesperson, either by offering them commission at the start, or finding the money to pay them later on. You could also be your own ad salesperson, even taking a job in the same field, or an internship just to learn the ropes and then apply them to your own fledgling publishing business. Although it may be easier, at least in the beginning while you are building up your blog to go with a specialist ad company like Federation Media or become part of a blog network.

AFFILIATES

Affiliate advertising is making money through commission on third party sales. Basically you have a link on a post or a page and if someone clicks through and buys it, you earn a commission.

There are a number of affiliate options out there. Affiliates can be a great way of making money and have the added benefit of allowing smaller blogs with less traffic a decent revenue, as long as they have a loyal reader base. They are a great advertising option because you don't need to have a lot of traffic to earn a decent living from affiliate networks. With affiliated advertising you include a link to a product on your site and then if someone clicks through and buys it you earn a commission. The amount can vary greatly. Some affiliate sites are great and others are not. The best way to make money through affiliate sales it by creating a good relationship with your readers. Build up their trust and never sell anything that you don't believe in and personally endorse. Never sell out. Ever. You want your readers to trust your opinion. The best way to earn good money is to have active and engaged readers. Some blogs are better to earn through affiliates than others. If your blog is about beauty then you could make really good money, if you blog about parrots, not as much.

Frost is with a few affiliates including Amazon. Amazon's commission varies from section to section but is generally about 5%. Frost gets a high click-through rate with Amazon.

There are other affiliates with better commission rates and as long as you are not just trying to sell your readers anything you can think of you should be able to make some money here and there.

The key to making money with affiliates is to make sure you recommend products you have genuinely reviewed and would recommend. Your readers trust you and won't like it if there are tons of affiliate links on your site and they end up buying something dodgy. Readers also don't like it when blogs sell out. We do book reviews at Frost and the link is usually to Amazon. We don't earn a ton of money if someone clicks through and buys a book (it ranges from 4p to 30p) but it is something and it all adds up in the end.

With affiliates, you get given a code which identifies your site and you use that, along with the code for the product, to link from your site to the product. This sounds harder than it is. It is generally very easy, especially with Amazon, where you just search for the product and then embed the code into your site.

Affiliates are a great way to earn money when you have a blog that doesn't have tons of traffic but does have a loyal readership. In fact, you could earn more money than a bigger blog because your readers trust you and your recommendations.

There are plenty of affiliate programs or networks to choose from. On top of that, most companies and brand have their own affiliate program. The opportunities for affiliate advertising are limitless. The good thing about this is that it won't be hard finding something that you truly love and can genuinely recommend to your readers. Always check what kind of commission rate they offer. Some are better than others. Pick networks with the most lucrative programs. Another good thing about affiliate networks is that you can join as many as you want. Make sure that any affiliate network you join is a great fit for your blog and your niche.

MERCHANDISE

If your blog really grows then you can sell merchandise such as T-Shirts, posters and mugs. You could get these from vistaprint.co.uk or cafepress.com. The added bonus is that the readers who buy these will be walking advertisements for you. Win win.

GO INTO DEEP LINKING.

Amazon: the percentage through Amazon affiliates program is actually quite low, 4-10 percent. Despite the lower percentage compared to other affiliate links, Amazon has a number of things going for it. The truth is, most people already shop on Amazon, have an account and trust it. When it comes to putting links on your blog it is very easy to do so. You just sign up to be an Amazon Associate and after you have, you just search for the product and then you can get a link for the product to put directly on your blog. You can choose to do this with an image or without. The best thing about Amazon is that it allows you to easily deep link to products. Deep linking is the best way to make money through affiliate sales. Taking customers straight to the product, page or category that they want, rather than having them search for the product by taking them to the site, means they are more likely to buy the item if they want to. Their interface is easy to use and they also have 24 hour cookies which means that if someone buys something, or even clicks to Amazon through your site and then buys a book, and a while later, something else, you will also earn commission on that. Handy for third party sales and means you can make easy money from someone spending a few hundred pounds on something just because they visited your site! Pretty cool. Amazon also sell pretty much everything you can think of, making it more likely that you will earn commission. Most people also have their payment details on Amazon and can pay for anything with one click.

If you are American then the bad news is that if you live in any of the following states, because of an online commerce tax law Amazon have discontinued their affiliate program. These are: Rhode Island, Arkansas, Colorado, Illinois, Minnesota and North Carolina. You won't be able to become an associate if you live in one of these states but Amazon are campaigning for nationwide legislation

AFFILIATE NETWORKS.

Affiliate networks are great because they tend to have a lot of brand and companies under one roof. Which usually happens is that you join the network and then you join the specific programs separately. This is handy because although you make money from a lot of different brands, you only have one log in, it is easy to manage and you get one payment from all of your sales instead of lot of little ones. It won't hurt to sign up to all of the different affiliate networks. This will let you know which ones will work for your site and which ones won't. If there is a specific brand that you want to work with then you need to find out which affiliate network they are with. If you have already signed up to all of the affiliate networks then hopefully you will already be with the network they are with. To find out which affiliate network the brand is with, go to their website and scroll down. They should have an affiliate link or a company information link that you can click on to get this information. If not, search online or ask some other bloggers. Especially if you know that they promote that brand.

AFFILIATES

- Affiliate Future

- OMG

- Affiliate Window: has UK and US brands.

- Buy.AT (specialise in gadget firms)

- LinkShare

- Commission Junction: this is one of the largest affiliate network out there. You can deep link to specific products and the interface is easy to use.

- ClickBank

- ShareaSale: has a lot of brands to choose from.

- PepperJam: smaller, has some good niche programs. Have heard it is friendly.

- eJunkie: particularly good if you want to promote ebooks online. This is a smaller network and is helpful to individual sellers.

- Rakuten Linkshare: also a large affiliate network. Have a unique bento box tool which allows for deep linking. Can do the same with their interface.

- CJ Affiliate

When choosing products always think about your readers and what they want. Never recommend something that is sub-par and don't recommend something just for the money. The best way to do affiliates is when you have personally reviewed something. This way the recommendation is backed up by personal experience. Make sure you don't just recommend things for the sake of it. You don't want your readers to think you are selling out.

Skimlinks is great because they send you a monthly report which shows which post was most clicked on your blog, how many times and how much you earned. It also has an area on the site where you can check out daily sales and such. I love it.

The longer cookies are active, the more likely you will get paid for a sale.

Swap the position of ads so regular viewers don't get used to them and just seem them as a design feature

According to research, 160 X 600 pixel skyscraper ads are the most clicked on and people also click on ads within content more than those outside it. Readers might find adverts within content annoying however as they might accidentally click on them. Always use your own discretion.

You can make adverts blend. Use the same colours and font as is in your blog. Or you could make them stand out. Try both and see what works for you.

When doing product reviews list the advantages and disadvantages.

Mix up size, font and colour. Make sure readers find your site useful.

Don't do too many advertorials. One a week is good.

Ad position is important. Check what is working and not.

Recommend products that your readers need.

Always have a good attitude.

Always update your media package and make sure it is clear and concise. Include graphs and charts. You need the number of uniques, impressions and views. Start with how many people you reach. Include social media followers and demographics. Use press cuttings and testimonials. Make sure you include your contact details. Include any links to good press you have gotten.

Do a survey and ask your readers lifestyle questions. Offer them a competition prize for doing the survey. The more you know about your readers the better.

Cut out the middle man. Sell your own advertising. Believe you can do it. Make a list of your blog's achievements and list your uniques. List endorsements and awards.

If you want to check out some media packages from successful blogs than you can scroll down and click on the 'advertise' link. You can do this for The Huffington Post, Perez Hilton and Techcrunch. Make sure you put a package together before you approach advertisers. Always be prepared. Don't waste anyone's time.

Have a realistic starting price in mind. This will stop you wasting both your time and theirs if they cannot afford you.

It would be easier to sell four smaller priced ads than one £2000 one. Less pressure too. Try to find out what other bloggers are charging. Make sure your price matches other bloggers of your size, if advertisers can get what they want for less money elsewhere then they will and if they can get the same traffic for less money they will. Have a look at what size of adverts other bloggers are using and what CPM they charge.

It is better to start low and then raise your prices as you become more popular.

Have a long list of advertisers and go through them all. Convince advertisers of the benefits of advertising online.

Look at who is advertising on Google AdSense and contact them directly. Look at other blogs and see who is advertising with them. Visit industry events and trade fairs. Contact brands and companies you have already written about.

Think of why an advertiser would advertise with you then use that to pitch to them. Let them know how they can benefit from advertising with you. Let them know that you can reach the people they want to reach. Think about what they want and need and how you can help them get it. The brand might need you for one of the following reasons: they are launching a new product, they want to change the perception of their brand, they want to reach a specific demographic or they want to increase their sales.

Emails are more convenient than telephone calls. People are busy. Always respect their time.

Have a draft email in a word document and copy and paste. Tailor each one to the individual advertiser. Be clear and concise. State the facts: about your blog, your brand, your traffic and what you can do for their business. With the third paragraph, tailor this to each business. This should be very easy to do and you can also do it quickly. Get the direct email address of the right person. Do your research.

Think about the advertisers' needs. After an advertiser is interested you can meet them in person, with a phone call or do it all over email. If you meet in person then make sure you are the best ambassador for your blog. Look good, dress well and be polite and professional. Hold your nerve, you have something to offer. Print your media package off and hand it to the advertiser. Tell them what other advertisers have advertised with you. Especially if they are in the same niche.

Offer a discount to advertisers who give you repeat business. This will make your life easier and save you time. You can offer packages month-to-month or on a 6 month or yearly basis. Make loyalty pay off. If an advertiser does show an interest in a long-term advertising package then you can offer an incentive like a month's free trial to seal the deal. If you deliver they will be delighted and you will get some of the pressure taken off.

Sell add-ons. Ask if they would like some other type of advertising while you are there. An ad in your newsletter, a sponsored post or branding at an event you are doing.

Have different pricing options.

Payment. Make an agreement at the time of closing the deal how the advertiser will pay. Either by PayPal, cheque or BACS. Do this when they are still enthusiastic about advertising rather than weeks later when they will be less excited. You don't want to have to sell the whole thing to them again.

After a while contact them and ask how they are getting on. Always give the personal touch. This will make you stand out from other brands and they may also recommend you to other people and work with you again. Always go the extra mile.

Believe in yourself. Communicate.

Direct sales alone may not make you wealthy from blogging. Many bloggers only earn about half of their income from advertising on their blog. You can also do public speaking and special projects.

When it comes to affiliate programmes, the best way to make money is to do deep linking. Deep linking is when you directly to the product, not just the site it is on. This saves your readers having to search for the product. Convenience is key. People don't tend to like being sold to, but if you can solve a problem that they have or offer some entertainment then they will be happy and will also buy from your site again.

Keep an eye on what sells and what doesn't. Again, give your readers what they want. If people are buying a certain type of product then do more reviews of that product. Treat your blog like a business. Track sales and experiment where the link should be positioned and what kind of wording works too.

Provide a disclaimer that you use affiliates either in the footer of the post, or in a general disclaimer somewhere on your site.

WAYS TO BOOST AFFILIATE SALES.

- Provide good content.
- Make sure you are sharing something of value.
- Make sure links are relevant and useful.
- Share links for things you actually like and would use.
- Share products from shops you actually buy from.

Mumsnet do a great thing where they get readers to share things that they love and recommend. This does not come across as spam or as if you are being sold to, you can tell these are genuine recommendations about products that have enhanced these people's lives. Try to do the same thing for your site. Share products that you love, that you use every day and would recommend to your friends. Promote and link to the products you truly love, that you are proud to be associated with. I always recommend books that I love. More so, because I want other people to read them than just to make money.

Pay attention to what your readers are buying. This will let you know what type of things they are interested in; helping with future blog posts, but also let you know what to link to in the future.

Give people an alternative. If you bought something from a local store then say so, but also offer an alternative they can buy through one of your affiliate programs. Giving them the choice shows that the recommendation is genuine.

Do gift lists, review lists and shopping guides. For every special occasion: Christmas, Valentine's Day, Mother's Day, Father's Day etc. We do a gift list. This is actually a tremendous amount of work, especially at Christmas which is a popular time for people to buy things. We get sent hundreds of things, all of which need to be reviewed and put into specific lists. I noticed that these were hugely popular and that they had a good click-through rate. People were buying what we were recommending. Even if you do not get sent a lot of stuff, it is work doing gift and shopping guides, as well as reviews. People love recommendations and always search for reviews before they buy things. You can do lists of products, don't overdo them but do so when you can genuinely recommend products and the list will benefit the reader. Give a unique spin on your shopping guides: "The Best X under £10", "The best family films" etc. That type of thing will work well and tends to be popular.

Make sure links are always relevant. Links should be contextual and always relevant to the post. Help the reader solve a problem, don't just sell them something

If you have a huge archive you can repurpose old posts. Take the popular older posts and add images or graphics, update your content and add new affiliate links that fit and don't look out of place. In the traditional publishing world repurposing old articles is called 'topping and tailing'.

Share deals and sales with your readers. Amazon and Skimlinks both either send their affiliates information on sales and deals to share, or have that information on the affiliate section of their site. Sharing a deal or a sale with your reader which they would not otherwise know about is a great way to make readers happy and earn a bit of money. Make sure the deal will be relevant to your reader. Again, know what your readers want.

Link to hard-to-find products and ingredients for recipes or supplies for DIY projects.

Sell things that are clogging up your home that you have previously reviewed. This obviously won't work with makeup and things that are used but gadgets and clothes can earn you a bit of money and will help declutter too.

SUBSCRIPTIONS.

Subscriptions are gold because rather than getting paid for a one off thing you continuously make money. That doesn't mean that signing people up for things is easy. There is so much free stuff on the internet that you really have to offer something that is either unique or has tremendous value. Or both. You could do this with a private forum, a jobs board, or online training courses. You would need to have exclusive content and be an expert in the chosen area to pull this off too.

DONATIONS.

If you have a loyal readership and other types of adverting aren't for you then you can ask your readers for donations. It is easy to place a donate button on your site. This does work for some blogs. Try the 'Buy me a beer' plugin. It's a different way to show a PayPal Donation Button. Not everyone will like a donate button, seeing it as asking for money, but donating tends to make people feel good and if your blog adds value to their lives they will probably donate. This technique would probably not work if you also have other types of advertising on the blog too.

CLASSIFIEDS.

You could also have classifieds on your blog. You could charge people to advertise jobs, rooms, things for sale etc.

INDIRECT INCOME.

All of your money does not need to come from your blog. Your blog is a great advertisement for you and your skills. Especially the more popular it gets. This makes you a 'name' in your industry and can get you indirect income from your blog.

SOURCES OF INDIRECT INCOME:

FREELANCE WRITING.

The more you get known as a writer the easier it will be to make money writing for other blogs and publications. When you first start off the money won't be great. You genuinely have people who want people to write 600 word articles for £15 including research, and others who offer $10! It can be worth doing this in the beginning to make a bit of money and learn the ropes but don't undersell yourself, especially as your reputation and talent grows.

If you get a byline and the work is for a good blog or publication it really does add to your brand. It is also great publicity. If a link to your blog is included, even more so. As your reputation grows and people read your work you will find that more work comes to you

You can also advertise your services on your blog. Make it clear to people that you are also a writer for hire. Have a page on your blog stating so and reference that you are a freelance writer in your posts and sidebar if you think it fits. Make your freelance ability known.

Some sites where you can find freelance writing work:

- elance.com
- jobs.problogger.net
- odesk.com
- performancing.com
- jobs.freelanceswitch.com
- craigslist.com
- gumtree.com

- freelancewritinggigs.com

Ask around; let people know you are looking for writing work.

Writing forums are also good places to find work and get the word out. You can meet like-minded people, network, get word-of-mouth jobs and let people know your availability.

Guests posts are a great idea as they can lead to paid work. They get your name and talent out there. Just make sure you are properly attributed and that you reference that you are a freelance writer who is available for work. A link to your blog should also be included.

When you start looking for writing work make sure you have plenty of work on your blog that you can show them. Also make sure it is diverse and shows your talent off well. If there is a specific publication you want to write for then write a post in the style of that publication and send the link to them. It will also help if you have basic SEO skills, know WordPress and have a high following that you can share the piece you write with. These things all add value to your writing brand and are more likely to get you hired. Show people why they should hire you over someone else.

For freelance writing payment types differ. Some will want to pay you per thousand words and others will pay per-post. You might only get $20 when you are starting out (and I use dollars because most sites which have freelance writing work are American and pay in dollars. Depressingly, even the ones in the United Kingdom have people who pay in dollars as it is a way to pay people less as the dollar is worth less than the pound), but you should soon build this up and earn ten or twenty times that amount.

It is worth asking who will own the content, when payment will be paid and if you will have to supply your own images. Some writing will also mean a lot of research so factor this into the price you charge. It is all well and good being paid by word but if it requires hours or days of research then it just won't be worth it.

PRINT MAGAZINES AND NEWSPAPERS.

Becoming an expert in your field is a huge asset for a writer. As is having something original to say. The vast majority of very successful writers that I know have their own niche. Jay Rayner is a restaurant critic who writes about food, Caitlin Moran is political and a feminist. She tends to write about feminism and women's issues with a measure of politics thrown in. If you think about the successful writers that you know, they tend to be known primarily for one thing. So becoming an expert in a certain field and writing about it prolifically will vastly improve your writing career and chances of getting hired.

Print magazines will be more interested in hiring someone with a successful blog as they already have an audience. Email editors for their submission guidelines or try to find out this information online. Signing up to Gorkana can also help you find work. They also have the contact details of editors and other journalists. They also send out an email alert of people who have been hired or have moved jobs, along with their contact details of them and the person who is replacing them.

EBOOKS AND BOOKS.

It is rather obvious that I know about this as you are reading my book right now! The good thing about books is that they become a passive income. This book is my third book and I have already started on my fourth. The first one was about how to be a successful actor and the second one was about wedding planning. I have promoted both on my blog by writing relevant posts on each subject. The key is to offer value. I do a lot of research and only write about what I know. I then pass that knowledge on to other people so they can advance their careers or plan their weddings.

Writing a book is not easy. It takes a substantial amount of work and research. It can be boring hard work but when it is finished and published you get a feeling like no other. I am happy with my book sales so far. That does not mean that you just hit publish and then the sales roll in. Like anything else, you need to get the word out, writing guest posts and sharing your books on social media. Quite a few people don't recommend publicising books on social media but I have to disagree because I have sold a few this way. Don't bombard people, though, and always be respectful. No spam.

After I have written a book I publicise it on my blog (as you should, it is a huge advantage to have your own blog. You already have an audience) but I also write guest posts on the subject of each book for The Huffington Post and others. Each promotion generally leads to some book sales and gets my name out there. The other thing about writing a book is that people will then take you seriously as a writer. Many people talk about writing a book but not many do. It is a huge achievement and will most likely get you more paid writing work in the future, as well as greatly adding to your brand.

Writing a book gives you prestige. After I wrote my acting book I was invited to write for different publications and was also interviewed on national radio. Not bad at all.

I think that every blogger should have an e-book. You already have the content and it is already being read. It makes sense to make it into a book. You can even rework some of your old, popular content and then make it into an e-book.

I self-publish my e-books through Amazon Kindle Direct Publishing (KDP) and I also put them on Smashwords. It is very easy to publish through Amazon Kindle Direct Publishing and they also have another option called CreateSpace which allows you to publish your books in print. Create-Space is easy to work, friendly and very reasonably priced. Amazon have made it easy for authors to publish their books and the Kindle market really has exploded over the past few years. There are even a number of Kindle millionaires. It is actually very easy to publish books through KDP so don't let that put you off. The other benefit of publishing with Amazon is that they are a powerful retailer. When people buy books, they tend to buy from Amazon. This gives you a great opportunity to reach people. People also trust Amazon and will have probably already bought something from it, so will be more likely to buy again.

If you don't want to go the Amazon route then you can do your e-book in a PDF version. This won't be that hard and probably be done on your computer. There is also an affiliate company called eJunkie that lets authors set up an affiliate program which allows other bloggers to earn commission from selling your e-book on their site.

SELF-PUBLISHING EBOOKS

Another good thing about self-publishing on Amazon is that users tend to already have their payment details on the site and can buy with just one click.

Google Documents format fits the specification to upload your book to Amazon's KDP. You won't need to modify the format which is handy. Keep in mind however that if you have just copied and pasted your book from your blog that Amazon scans the internet to make sure your book is not available free elsewhere. Rewrite posts but you should also add a lot of other information too. You don't want to just copy and paste stuff from your blog. Offer value and make sure your book is worth the readers' time and money. You don't want to sell an awful product or make people feel like they were ripped off.

Market your book by blogging on topics that are related to it and then adding a link to the book in the post. Email your subscribers, letting them know that you have a new book out or include an advertisement to it on the sidebar of your blog. You can even do this via your Amazon Affiliate links. Just embed the code and that makes it easier.

Get good reviews. This is particularly important on the Amazon page. Most people won't buy a book with no reviews and certainly not with a lot of bad ones. Get as many good reviews as you can and ask people to leave the reviews on Amazon too. Good reviews also improve your search rank on Amazon. This is valuable as people will search for certain type of books on Amazon. If yours comes up and has good reviews then it is more likely to be bought.

Do guest posts and link back to your book. I write for the amazing Huffington Post and always tend to sell a few books when I write an article for them. You can take it further by doing content marketing on various platforms. If your book is about self-confidence you could do YouTube videos and mention your book on them, you could answer questions on Quora about self-confidence and link back to your book, speak at conferences or events and...you guessed it, mention your book. You could also do a podcast about self-confidence and plug your book at the end. You could even contact local radio stations and media to see if they will review your book, feature or interview you. The same with national media.

You can have pretty much anything done for $5 using fiverr.com

You will also need a book cover. Both Amazon KDP and CreateSpace let you create free book covers with their cover creation tools. They say people judge a book by its cover and it is very true. The better the cover, the more likely you are to sell copies. Spend a bit of time on it.

Some people will find writing a book harder than others but keep at it. The first e-book will be hard but it will be worth it in the end. Even if you just write a few hundred words a day.

The good thing about having a blog is that you will already have a lot of content. You will obviously have less if you are just starting out but Frost has a bank of thousands of articles and a significant number of those were written by me. I wrote about acting before I published my acting book and the same about weddings, so when I started writing these books I was already used to writing about the subject, had already done some research, and even had one or two articles that could be rewritten and incorporated into the book.

Another way to make money is to help other writers with their books. Either with some articles you have written on the topic or with your knowledge in that specific field. As your reputation grows you may even find yourself being approached by writers.

Approach traditional publishers. Do your research. See what publishers have published books from bloggers before, especially ones in your niche. Look at other bloggers' books and check who has published them and then contact those publishers. After you have found out the publishers' name head to their website for their submission guidelines. All publishers have them. Follow them to the letter and then be patient. It will probably take them a while to get back to you.

As you start writing more books have a 'by the same author' page.

SPECIAL PROJECTS.

Make sure you are known by all of the PR companies in your subject matter. Contact PR companies and let them know who you are and what you do. Sell yourself. Print off your Google Analytics and show them how amazing your blog is. When they see who you can reach they will remember you when they want to meet that specific target.

If you want to sell your blog one day you have to keep growing it. People buy a blog for its potential. Millions of followers, good revenue and growth potential is what you need. Sell at the right time.

To find out the PR company of a certain brand you want to work with you can email or call their head office. Then ask the receptionist. You could also ask other bloggers or journalists. Some companies do their own PR and other have external PR companies. A search engine might get you the information.

Gorkana will also put you on their directory for free. As will the Diary Directory. PR people will then contact you and send you invites and press releases. You can also pay a subscription to sign up to Fashion Monitor (fashionmonitor.com). If your niche is fashion it will give you access to a lot of media contacts. The Media Eye is another site you can sign up to.

Contact PR companies.

Join Facebook groups where other bloggers hang out.

Read up on publishing laws.

Be ambitious and believe in yourself.

Set targets.

Get mentioned in the press.

Enter blog competitions like the Cosmo Blog Awards or the UK Blog Awards.

Ask to guest edit blogs.

Independent Fashion Bloggers is a great site for blogging in general and for those with a fashion niche. They do a lot of good posts on blogging.

Wear clothes from a brand that you have an affiliate with and take lots of pictures. Call in products and make sure you can personally recommend them.

CONSULTING.

Doing consulting work, either on blogging, writing or the niche subject your blog is about is a good way of earning money. When you become an expert in your field people will come to you for advice and help. If you offer consultation work then make it clear in your blog in the about me page or services page. People cannot hire you if they don't know you are in the market for something. You could also have a banner in your sidebar stating what services you offer. Give examples and let people know what makes you qualified to do the work. You could even include a PayPal button so people can pay in advance. This saves you chasing clients for payment and protects you from non-paying clients, the bane of every freelancer's life.

Some points to remember. You can:

- Reach out to brands for private advertising and sponsored content.
- Do ad networking advertising.
- Make money through affiliate links.
- Maximise ad revenue on your site. Work directly with brands. You can also do freelance writing for other sites.
- Make money from speaking fees.

- Make money by online consulting, consulting in person or teaching something.
- Do social media consulting.
- E-books, online courses, videos and e-resources are all good ideas for earning money.
- Networking and building business partnerships is important.
- Sponsorship is a good option.
- You can do live events. Many blogs have their own events now, like mashable.com for example.

YOUTUBE.

Vlogging is huge and many people have become rich by doing YouTube videos. Debbe Djordjevic from Handpicked Media gave me this advice when I wanted to expand Frost Magazine: "Don't go to print, go to YouTube." Becoming a YouTube partner can earn you thousands. In fact, it has made a number of people millionaires.

How you make money with your blog will probably be a mixture of sources, and if you want to take it seriously as a business you really should have a mixture. What is right for you and your blog will not be the same for other people. Although it does pay to check out how the competition is making money. Always be on the lookout for new ways to monetise and keep checking what is working and not working. Think outside the box. As time goes by you may find you are making enough money through affiliates and don't need to take sponsored posts anymore. This is your call. Trust yourself and make your own smart business decisions.

SELLING YOUR BLOG.

If you make a success of your blog someone might want to buy it from you. Many people buy and sell blogs. Some people even buy blogs to flip (sell) them. This might be another way for you to make blogging a business: buying and selling blogs. Blogs that get thousands of hits every month are worth money, remember this. You can sell your blog at Digital Point or SitePoint.

Buying and selling blogs for a profit.

You could also buy a blog. The reasons to buy a blog are the following: it already has a proven track record, readers, traffic, subscribers etc. To start a blog, build an audience and gain traffic takes a significant amount of time and effort. So buying can be worth it. However, whilst starting a blog is relatively cheap, buying one can be very expensive. Make sure you do a lot of research before buying a blog. Ask people you trust for their opinion. Financial investments can go either way and there is no promise of a profit. Another thing to factor in is that the readers may not like the blog being taken over. Loyalty is as easily lost as it is won. Buying a blog is risky and it could go either way. If the blog has some regular writers that the audience love then try and keep them on, this should make the transition go more smoothly. Also be aware that when you buy an old blog you also buy its baggage, the only way for a blog to be yours entirely is to build one yourself.

A blog's value is held in the money it generates, the traffic and uniques, the content, resale value, influence and future potential. The older a blog is the better, not just because of SEO but also because it has grown an audience and lasted. Make sure the traffic and success of the blog has been steady and shown growth. When buying a blog, have a long term business goal in mind. Don't just step into it blindly or without a plan. A blog which has not had lots of owners is not as good as one that has had one. Negotiate hard, especially when buying to flip. In business the best advice is always to buy low and sell high. You may also want to get a contract or put the money in escrow. It is all well and good keeping things friendly but this is business and you probably won't know the person you are buying from personally. Be businesslike and don't take any risks. You don't want to get screwed over or have someone run off with your money.

Valuations are important when buying a blog. Even if you do not want to sell your blog, it is still a smart idea to value it. It lets you know how well you are doing and can also spur you on if the valuation is good. What adds to a blog's value is: good content (worth its weight in gold, ideas, talent and investment), registered users, good inbound links, forums, RSS feeds, social media followers and accounts, email subscribers and audience. Blogs with a rich audience will obviously attract more money. Businesses also tend to buy blogs that rank well for search terms that are important to their business. This may sound silly but will be much cheaper than paying for an expensive SEO expert.

When buying a blog make sure you know what you are getting. You should get all of the content and the social media accounts too. Also make sure the content is original and included. Make sure you know what you are getting and have it put in writing. Also ask to see their Google analytics. They may inflate their traffic; you want to know exactly what you are paying for. Analyse any stats and graphs they give you thoroughly and reach your own conclusions. Make sure the traffic is not just to one or two articles but is spread amongst the entire site. You want the traffic to be genuine.

Make sure the blog is earning a profit and that that profit is from diverse sources. Double, no, triple check there are no debts associated with the blog. Buying a blog which is a brand is a good idea, but make sure you can carry that brand forward.

Always do a background check on the person you are buying from. Use whois.domaintools.com, archive.org and search engines to find out as much as you can. Like any business deal, don't go into it blind. Find out as much information as you can.

You can buy to flip or buy to reap the benefits. If you buy a blog to flip it then make sure there is a market for that blog. Having some potential buyers already lined up, or at least researched is prudent and will pay off in the long term. People you could sell to include companies in the niche of the blog who want the audience and traffic that the blog will have, competitors and other bloggers who want to expand.

Another thing to take into consideration is tax. It will probably pay off in the long run to get the advice of an accountant.

- Always have your business brain switched on. It goes without saying, but watch out for scams.
- Another thing a blog gives you is influence, and influence is very important and cannot be bought.
- Think about strategy. Have focus and a vision.
- Always be businesslike.

If you choose a niche, choose a niche that you love, not just one that you think will make money. Choosing a subject that you won't get bored off is one of the smartest decisions you can make. Blogs require a lot of effort and writing about a subject you hate will only make you miserable.

You can track the progress of your blog via alexa.com and seomoz.org/tools. It is not completely accurate and our Google Analytic account gives better data. Alexa always seems to think Frost is doing worse than it is. Bad Alexa.

CHAPTER 3: CONTENT. WHAT TO WRITE ABOUT AND GIVING READERS WHAT THEY WANT

The first rule of blogging is: content is king. And it is a fact. You need good content to get people reading and to keep people reading. The sad fact is that you can write the best article in the world and it won't find an audience. Some posts flop and others, in which you have less emotional input, will get thousands of hits. In this chapter we will go into writing quality content and how to get it read.

Start with your audience. Find out what they want and give it to them. Make sure your content is unique and that it serves a purpose. Whether that be entertainment or educational. Give your readers as much amazing content as possible. Other people may also do what you do but you do it your way. Write about what you love, what you are passionate about. Write about something that excites you.

Before you launch your blog make sure you write some flagship content. Give people something to read.

Tips

- *Google likes sites that are updated regularly.*
- *Blog consistently. At least a few times a week. This keeps people returning to your site.*
- *Do a lot of research into your subject.*
- *Do FAQs. (Frequently asked questions)*
- *Jargon busters.*
- *Case studies.*
- *Meet a need.*
- *Do a call to action. Whether that be to subscribe to your newsletter or comment on the post.*

- *Write down good headlines as they come to you.*

- *Think about what you would want to read.*

- *Share what you know.*

- *Follow trends and the latest product launches. Be relevant and up-to-date.*

- *Use an informative and friendly tone.*

Don't be too vague. Let people know what the article is about. Make sure all headlines are under 140 characters as this means search engines index it better and it improves SEO.

Don't just review anything. You will lose followers and waste your time.

Always remember that you are doing the company a favour when reviewing. Your blog is worth something, as is your time and effort. Don't get so obsessed with doing reviews that you forget to be creative.

You need the interesting ideas. Make it beautiful, compelling and make sure it solves a problem or informs. Blogging is fast and immediate. Build up a community for your readers.

DO GIVEAWAYS

The easiest way to get your blog known is by making influential people aware of it. Pulling your resources and networking like a demon.

Make sure the article is worth posting. Don't post too much. People won't have time to read it. Quality is more important. If it's amazing it goes in. You can cover club nights and live nights. You can review books and albums. Contact record labels.

Interact with people. Update at least three times a week. Do collages. Experiment with new visuals and storytelling ideas. If you feature a celebrity send coverage to the celebrities' agent. If writing about a specific celebrity then put a link to your article on their Facebook fan groups. Take the law seriously. You are liable for mistakes. Don't libel anyone and always check your facts.

Google sees someone else linking to your site as a vote of confidence. This improves your SEO.

If you have a problem, blog about it and ask your readers for their advice.

Get someone to handle ad sales when you start out so you can focus on building good content. Selling advertising is time-consuming and requires expertise. Of course there will be a financial outlay so you could always go with Google AdSense instead.

If you haven't done anything wrong, try to hold steady when threatened with legal action. If you haven't done anything, you haven't done anything.

HERE ARE SOME ARTICLE IDEAS AND TIPS:

- Do cook-alongs if you have a food blog.
- Stay on top of your game. Keep the quality high.
- Always show personality.
- Keep information at a high standard. Offer people something no one else does.
- The more content the better but don't over post. You may lose readers this way. Schedule articles.
- Good content always wins in the end.
- Take time off. Don't spend all day every day at your computer
- There must always be something more about what you do. Be different.
- Review stuff that is already within reach until you have built your blog up enough to get sent product.
- The more value you offer the more likely people will be to come back.
- Show your personality. Be authentic.
- Don't include fluff or flowery writing in your posts. The more you write, the better you will get.
- Share your own experiences. Human beings like to connect with each other emotionally.
- Start strong. Have a good opening that draws people in.
- Bullet point the key points in your article to make it easier for the reader to process.
- Do a short paragraph which summarises the post. Include some good closing remarks. Give a clear conclusion.

- Use sub headings: they make posts more readable and they look more organised. It also improves SEO.
- Write regularly and with consistency.
- Posts that start with "how to" or "5 tips" are popular. Target your content to an audience who is likely to share. Get your audience to spread the word.
- Particular things are more likely to get shared than others. Infographics, beautiful videos that tell a story and collections of facts that challenge assumptions.
- Let other people use your images under the condition that they link back and credit you. Put this under your image, in your terms and conditions or have this information in your sidebar. You can find people who use your image and don't link back by using the Image Search Function on Google Images for "similar images" Google will then show you other images that it thinks look like yours. Contact the person not linking and ask them very nicely for a link. Always be polite. Don't burn bridges. Maybe you will make a friend.
- Don't give up. Some days will be hard. Barrel through and it will be worth it in the end.
- Set yourself targets.
- Always ask if your readers would be interested in this.
- Keep your readers feeling valued and they will keep coming back.
- If you want to attend a specific event then do a quick right up about it and then go to the events website and find the contact us section to contact the PR department for press accreditation. Call their head office if you can't find the PR details. Be pushy and determined.
- Number and quality of readers is important. Create content that will attract a regular readership.
- Have a lot of contributors. Make sure they are all of a high quality.
- Become established. Build a community where a number of writers can all contribute. These could be things like recipes or something else. The more people writing, the better. Make them all feel a part of it. Like The Huffington Post.
- Product placement is a possibility but make sure it is something you believe in and recommend personally.
- Have a USP. Try new things.
- Keep your tone consistent.
- You can also use keywordtool.io to come up with popular, searchable ideas. Keywords are very important when writing content.
- Use a good title and then write high quality content about the subject.
- Use links, not static text. Links improve SEO. Validate your facts by linking to other information.

- Have a special edge that no one else has thought of. Specialise.
- Keep the quality of content to a high standard.
- Remember that with blogging you have to work very hard to get very little back for a long time. Don't get discouraged.
- Be accountable for what you write. Never make things up and hold true to your beliefs.
- Have a great persona and build a great brand within your niche.
- PRs, journalists and writers search the web looking for good sites. If yours is of a high standard then they will be interested. Write newsworthy stories and be original. This will get you more content and could get your story in the mass media.
- If you get the same question over and over again then write a post about it.
- Build up trust with your readers and PR people. Always put your readers first and always be honest.
- Learn about upcoming releases. These could be music or movies releases.

To find popular conversations Mediagazer, WeSmirch, PopURLs, Memeorandum, Alltop and Topsy are all good.

Do a list of the best in your niche and analyse their content. Analyse blogs, Twitter, people and Facebook pages. Go to conferences. Write about them and let the people who attended and did talks know afterwards.

Have a unique angle.

Reach out to other blogs. If they like you they might link to you.

Listen to feedback. Treat social media as a two-way conversation.

Always meet your readers' needs. Experiment and innovate. Don't just mimic other blogs.

Post better and quicker. Be interactive with your community.

Readers generally like money-saving posts. Ways to make money and special offers tend to be popular. You could feature cashback websites and articles on selling on eBay.

In regard to your personal life, think about what you put out there. You can't get your privacy back. Be careful about blogging about your family. You don't want an HR company Googling your children in 15 years' time and finding your blog. Just because you write about parenting doesn't mean you have to write about your children in an overtly personal way.

Be careful of press embargoes. Never break them. It will ruin your reputation. A lot of the time when you get sent a press release there will be an embargo on the date you can feature it. Feature it before and you break the embargo, opening yourself up to a whole host of problems.

HARO (Help A Reporter Out) is an organisation through which you can respond to reporter queries. Gorkana is another one. Build relationships.

Press trips are always fun. I went to Toulouse and my writer, Holly, went to Jerusalem. Press trips are all-inclusive free trips to a destination or place.

Always fact check and do your research.

Updating 3-5 times a week is best.

Family days out and craft activity are good post ideas if they suit your blog.

Celebrity Tweets (celebritytweets.com) have all of the celebrities' tweets in one place. This can be a great source for inspiration and also for connecting with celebrities.

You learn to write by reading. Read books, magazines and other blogs.

Keep an eye on blogging trends.

Start small. Make sure you write every day. Force yourself even if you do not feel like it.

Set goals and have a schedule.

Write the conclusion first if you are struggling.

Attend and write about an event.

Interviews are a great way to create good content. You have to write the questions and then the rest is done by the interviewee. Reasons to interview people: they are easy. You just have to do the questions, you will be helping out the person you interview, if you can get a high profile person you will look well-connected, it is a great way to meet people and much nicer than just taking up their time and the interview can really add to your prestige if it is a good one with high-quality answers. It could even be picked up by other bloggers or the national mainstream media. I prefer doing email interviews because transcribing is one of the least fun things you can do in life.

If there is a need for information, give it to people.

Do what is working, write something similar but from a specific perspective.

List resources. The best ..., the worst ..., the funniest...., for example.
Summarise a book or a film.

Give your opinion.

Have an archive so people can easily find your old content.

Write with passion. Use your knowledge and experience

Create a sense of community.

Make your posts wow and readable.

Don't just post something for the sake of it. Focus on writing good content and promoting it. One good article is worth hundreds of sub-par ones.

Slow and steady wins the race.

Checking spelling and grammar is vitally important. A lot of bloggers use Grammarly. If you cannot afford a proofreader then it will pay off to do a proofreading course yourself. Try to make your grammar and spelling as good as they can be. It will make your blog look more professional. It will also stop annoying comments from readers pointing out the one spelling or grammar mistake on the post you have spent days writing.

Do a deals of the week post. Let readers know about bargains. Approach PR companies for competition goods to giveaway. Do a competition where you give something away every day. This builds readers and loyalty.

Ask the right questions to get your readers commenting on your blog. Start conversations and make a sense of community.

Competitions: Ask readers to leave the answer in the comments. Incentivise people. I get hundreds of comments on my blog when I do a competition. Don't feel too bad if your blog does not get a lot of comments. Every other blogging book seems obsessed with comments, and I know that it is a great thing for your blog but in my experience people do comment a lot...on other social media sites. My articles get comments on Reddit and Facebook and Twitter. In my opinion, people rarely leave comments on blogs anymore. They do it on their social media account where their friends will see it so their friends give their opinion and they feel like they have shared. Make sure readers know you are grateful for comments. Offer competition prizes and thank them personally. Tell them how much you loved their comments. Run more competitions. Competitions always get lots of comments. Join in, leave comments and even post links to other relevant articles the reader might be interested in. Always respond to comments that people leave on your blog. Unless it is from a troll, then block and ignore.

Every time I did a competition on my blog I noticed a spike in traffic come from moneysavingexpert.com It turns out they have a competition section on their forum and someone had posted the competition there. This happens every time I do a competition now so I would recommend joining Money Saving Expert and putting your competition details on. Another site that also does this is loquax.com People are very serious about entering competitions and for some it is what they do for a living and they enter competitions every day. Put your competition on the two sites which advertise new competitions and watch your traffic go up.

You can even run special offers for your readers. Run them for a limited time and target them to your audience. If you do special offers as a long running thing then always do them on the same day so people know when to check in. Let people know about competitions and discounts via your social media channels. To do special discounts, find brands you want to work with. This could even be restaurants and bars. Pitch your site to them and they should be happy to give you a discount code for the product/place that your readers can use in exchange for the free advertising. After a while you can start charging companies for this service but make it free to start with just to drum up interest. You should even get companies approaching you to feature them as the momentum builds. Remember: all you do is supply the discount code, the company does the rest of the work, whether that is shipping products to customers or redeeming their code. It is up to the company to fulfil the order. When you first start doing this it is best to stay local and then branch out. Local stores and companies are more likely to say yes. Also pitch companies that you have already worked with and know.

To get started send a short email to the companies, include some readership statistics and mention what is in for them (free advertising). Say that it is free of charge. You should have a reasonable success rate.

Look through magazines to see who is advertising at the moment. Always make sure that things are relevant to your readers.

Use CAPTCHA (a challenge response test) to deter spammers. Akismet and Security Ninja are both good at stopping spam on your blog.

If you want to thank people for leaving a comment on your blog and you are on WordPress then you can use a plugin called Comment Relish.

Do web chats. You can use Google + hangouts to do this. Make people feel welcome and build a good reputation.

THE EDITORIAL CALENDAR

The editorial what? Basically this is something that newspapers and print publications use, and you should too. Each month has a range of things and events that you can write about on your blog or do posts on. For example: January has New Year Resolutions, February is Valentine's Day, March has Mother's Day, April has Easter, December obviously has Christmas. There are also the 'seasons' in London and culture. Summer means music festivals, autumn means art festivals. All of this gives you a lot of things to write about. At Frost we also do gift lists which are hugely popular. These are basically Valentine's Day, Father's Day, Christmas Gift lists. We put out a media alert on Gorkana and PR people will send us products to review from their clients. If we think the product is up to snuff then we will feature it in the gift list and recommend it to our readers, using affiliate links wherever possible to make a bit of money. Readers love them but so do PR people who get their clients' products some hard-to-get publicity. You won't necessarily get to keep the products however. Some of them will be loan samples. Weigh up if this will be worth it for you.

Print works three months in advance so you end up going to Christmas parties and press events in July and get Valentine's Day requests in December.

You can use the editorial calendar plug in for WordPress.

You may hate schedules, or just not want to write about particular things, that is fine but the editorial calendar can be helpful when you are stuck for something to write about and need some inspiration. Being organised can really mean the difference between a blog that does okay and one that is very successful.

PLANNING POSTS IN ADVANCE.

Planning posts in advance has a number of benefits. You can take a day off, you will always be working on something and you can take your time to create good content instead of rushing things every day.

Some bloggers work 3-4 months in advance. Yikes.

Brainstorming articles is always a good idea. Always write down ideas as they come to you. Setting some time aside to have a proper brainstorming session once a week is a very good idea.

Don't worry if you don't think you are a naturally gifted writer. The more you write, the better you will get.

Consider joining a writing group in your area. You should be able to find one on the internet.

Write a killer post: have one clear point. Write posts that evoke an emotional reaction. Make them easy to read. Good posts teach something.

Installing the WordPress Popular post plugin (or something like it) on your site will keep your good, popular posts being read by people who visit the homepage and may have otherwise missed it. Make the most of your back catalogue, not just your newer content. The more awesome posts you write, the more successful your blog will be.

Write every day. Even on days that you really don't want to. Try to write one piece of killer content a week at least. More if you can.

Make sure posts have a killer picture to go with them. (See the next chapter) That way they will get pinned on Pinterest and you will get more hits. Make sure your pictures are all pinnable. The more they are shared on Pinterest, the more hits you can get.

Tip: Never use a long word when a short one will do.

Be prepared for people to disagree with you.

Sign up to the Mumsnet blogging network. You don't need to be a mum. They have different categories for different blogs. Including food and feminism.

Taking some time off. Always important. Schedule some articles and off you go!

Always make sure you back up. Even more so if you put your articles straight into the draft section of your blog. You don't want to lose years of work and all of your amazing content.

TESTING YOUR SITE AND CONTENT

We live in a visual world and people have high expectations. Make sure your blog draws people in. No terrible design or awful pictures. Give your readers the whole package. Make sure your site is not too busy. Too much information, graphics and flashing advertisement puts people off. Make it professional-looking, stylish but also simple and easy to read.

Take a hard, brutal look at your site design. Is the design too garish or cluttered? Can readers find what they are looking for? Is the navigation good? Can people tell what your site is about? Is the font easy to read? Are the pictures high-quality? Does it leave a good impression? Ask friends and family for their honest opinion. Ask them if the navigation bar is easy to use and if they could find their way around easily.

There is a site called Peek which is a free user-testing site. They will send you a short video of someone using your site for the first time if you put in your URL and email address. I have never used it myself but some other people have recommended it. Always keep improving the user experience of your readers in mind. Keep your blog organised and cohesive. Make the navigation on your site very easy. Make sure that readers can easily find what they want to read. The easier you make your site to navigate, the more likely people will stay on it, find your amazing content, and read some more. As time goes by, remove categories that don't work, don't get read much or that you just can't find the passion to write about anymore. Keep your navigation bar concise and clear.

Think of ways to highlight your killer content. Make a button on your sidebar that highlights your great content. Make a popular post page and add a popular posts section to your sidebar.

You have to give people what they want. If you want to just write what you want then you might need to just have a personal blog. Of course, you may be lucky and your personal blog will just take off and gain lots of followers. The truth is: if you want your blog to be your business you are going to have to do your market research and give your customers what they want. That doesn't mean changing who you are or your niche, it just means sorting out what is popular and creating more of it. But how to find out what they want? There are a number of ways.

- Look at your most popular posts and give the readers more of the same. Then give them more of the same, but different.
- Surveying your readers or asking for feedback.
- Checking referral statistics. You should be able to see this on your WordPress on the same page as your site statistics under 'search engine terms'. Or use 103bees.com, which is a tool that tracks how people come to your blog. Under your site stats in WordPress you will also see 'referrers'. So you can see which sites people are coming to your site from.
- If a post gets lots of comments or shares then you should write on that subject more. It really adds to the value of your blog. Find out what people want and give it to them.
- Try and create unique content, if you provide something that no-one else does then that will help your blog gain readers. There are tens of millions of blogs, making yourself stand out from the crowd will gain you loyal readers. Distinguishing your blog from other blogs makes a huge difference.

MAKING YOUR POSTS EASY TO READ

Create scannable content. Your post must be readable. When people read online they read in less depth than they do when reading print. People also have short attention spans so keep that in mind. You can write long, in-depth articles but make sure you also have some fun, easy articles that your readers can read on their lunch break. Sometimes people only have five minutes and just want to be entertained.

To make your posts easy to read think of doing the following:

- Lists: readers love articles in list form. Especially online. Bulleted form or numbered lists are both popular.

- Formatting: make things easier to read by putting important points or people of note in bold. This makes the article easier to read but also grabs people's attention. Capitals, italics and underlining can also be used to make a post more readable and interesting. Do not go overboard however; you don't want to put readers off. Underlining can also mean words are a link so this might confuse readers.

- Use pictures to break up posts and long articles. People love pictures and a picture paints a thousand words. Putting pictures at the top of your post draws people in.

- Using headings and subheadings breaks up content and draws people to the rest of the post. These help with the structure of the post.

- Using block quotes also breaks up text and draw readers in.

- If you do an interview have the questions in bold and the answers in normal text. This makes the interview easier to read and catches people's interest..

- Short paragraphs help with longer posts. People reading online tend to find it hard to read large blocks of text.

- Use spaces well. Using spaces well will stop your readers feeling overwhelmed and make articles easier to read.

Always keep a notepad and pen handy or the notes section on your phone so you can write down any article ideas you get. Don't just think that you will remember them, there will always be some that slip from your memory and you will kick yourself. I have been annoyed at myself when I have not written down ideas and then forgotten them.

Read print publications and newspaper to get story ideas, not just other blogs and websites. You could also get great story ideas from TV and film. Either way, keep up-to-date with what is happening in the world and in the media/tech world in general.

- Always create valuable content.
- Be a problem solver, answer people's questions.
- Write posts between 500-1250 words in length.

If you are disorganised then create to-do lists of posts and then tick them off as you go. A successful blog requires discipline so do whatever you can to make your life easier.

Make your posts as easy as possible to read and your readers will stick with you. Combine great content with pinnable, beautiful pictures. Awesome content sells itself.

Pinterest. The image you share should have enough of the story and have a brilliant picture so people want to click over and read the rest immediately. Make sure your picture sells your story. Give a good enough description to an amazing picture and you will have people click through to read the full post. Combine amazing content, a great image, a graphic that works with the title, along with an engaging description and you will make people want to click through and read your post. Therefore: more traffic.

Try to write life-changing articles. Improve people's lives.

Fact: Blogging is only about fifteen years old!

Keep your traffic streams diverse. This way you won't get caught out and your blog will not get damaged if you lose that stream.

Focus on both long and short term growth.

Paid advertising, link parties and blog hops all help build traffic.

For reviews tell the history, the story and about the people behind a product. Don't be generic. Give your readers information. It is all about storytelling.

Get gig tickets, film tickets and go to film festivals,

Find out what is happening and ask to attend.

Subscribe to a diary planning service like Media Eye.

Make friends with photographers and you will get tip offs of what is happening. Keep in contact with them and talk to them at the event.

Contact every PR person, the more you know, the more invites you will get.

Contact film studios and record companies for free tickets. Let them know what you do. Contact their press office. Take the opportunity to network.

Be consistent with your style so that people start to know your brand and your style. They should be able to look at your content and know that is you and your brand. Make your style consistent by using the same font, colour and graphics.

TITLES

Always write your titles in title case. Title case means capitalising the first letter of every word that is over two letters. So The Title Would Look Like This. (The so is capitalised as it is the beginning of the sentence). You can capitalise the first letter of every word if you want, or those over three letters, make your own decisions on what you think looks best.

Writing good content is important but the title is just as important, if not more so because it is what makes people click on the link. A good title can mean the different between a post going viral or only getting ten hits. People have short attention spans and busy lives. There is so much content out there that getting people to click on a link can be very hard indeed. Getting your title right can get you to the top in search engines and grab the attention of readers who subscribe to your Twitter, Facebook or RSS feed.

Your title will be the only thing that readers can judge your content on social bookmarking sites like digg.com, delicious.com, stumbleupon.com and reddit.com. If you get the title right then the thousands of people on these sites will click through to your article to learn more.

Grab people's attention with a good title. Your post's title is basically an advertisement for it.

Keep paragraphs short. Make sure they are easy to read and punchy.

The posts will also contribute to your SEO. The permalink in your URL (uniform resource locator), the link that people click on to get to the post should have some keywords of what your post is about. This will put it higher up in search engines and let search engines know what the post is about, so then the post can be indexed properly.

The best titles are short and simple. If you keep the title under 40 characters then the whole title will fit into the search results in Google. Short titles are good for search engines.

At least give a suggestion of what the post is about

If your title meets a need that readers have then it will draw them in and also get to the top of social bookmarking sites. How to articles and ones that teach people something they want to know are always popular. Fix something in your reader's life or add to it in some way and you may be on to a winner. Make readers think that they need to hear what you have to say.

Give the reader a taster in the title. This will draw them in as they will want to know more. Be descriptive in your title without giving everything away.

Use good, descriptive keywords in your title. This helps with SEO. Apparently keywords near the beginning are more powerful than the ones at the end. This can seem hard, to keep the title short and contain useful keywords. It is doable so just try your best and add some words on what the article is about in the title.

So you want short and snappy with good keywords. It can be hard to do this and come up with good titles but no one said blogging was easy. Be descriptive with your titles and make sure you put as much effort into the title as you do writing the post, otherwise it may never get read. Think of your title as an advertisement for the blog post and ALWAYS spell check it and make sure there are no errors. I frequently put titles into a search engine just to spell check. I thought this was a weird quirk but quite a few of my writer friends do the same thing.

It is good to grab attention with a title. Whether through controversy, a claim or a debatable issue. An important thing to remember about titles is not to confuse or make false claims. Your post must match up to your title. If you click bait people and then they feel you wasted their time or tricked them with a post that is not what the title claimed or just inferior then they will feel cheated and won't come back to your site.

After you have thought about the title it is time to think about the post itself. Try and make your opening good. Include important facts, pictures or humour to catch the readers' attention and make them read all the way to the end.

- Write your headline first.
- Keep things simple, don't use too many big words. Keep away from puns and irony.
- Do your research when writing titles. Look at what other blogs and publications are doing. Think about what works and what doesn't.
- Bad comments are not better than having none at all.

If a reader notices a factual mistake or spelling or grammar error in one of your articles, thank them and then correct the mistake. If you updated a factual error then you can also add the correction at the bottom and add that the article has been updated.

Make the call to action obvious to the reader: 'Download NOW', 'Get a free copy', 'Add to cart', 'Join Now'. Adding the word "now" is good. Check out what bigger sites do as they will know what works. Use good button generator software. Use simple links for CTA (call to action) in articles because otherwise it just looks spammy.

If you have a business blog then don't just post something for the sake of it. Always have a purpose. Create graphics and make CTAs visible and eye-catching within your blog.

POST LENGTH

The best word count for posts on the internet is hotly debated. But between 250 and 1000 words is the general consensus. Obviously the shorter the article the more posts you can write but you also need to offer your readers something meaty to get their teeth into. The best thing is to not over-write, say what is needed and then no more. Plenty of popular blogs churn out short pieces and it works for them. Check your stats and see what is popular and working, then give your readers some more of that. Keep each post focused on one topic. Don't go off on a tangent. If you have a lot to say then break it down into various posts. You can even link them together if you want, but don't confuse readers with a post which is trying to say too many different things. Interestingly, I write for the Huffington Post and they do not accept posts that are less than 500 words. Considering they are one of the top blogs in the world, if not the top one, there is probably something in that

HOW OFTEN SHOULD YOU POST?

Post frequency. This is another hot topic in blogging. How often should you post? Again, there is no straight answer. Some people don't like to get swamped in new posts from their favourite blog, others want constant updates. What you want is the middle ground. What do people want?

Well at this point it is less important what people want. Unless you start your blog with a friend or have some great friends that will write for you frequently it is very important that you do not burn yourself out. This will damage your health and also make you hate blogging. That is not what you need. I have not followed my own advice in the past but I always do now. If you need a break then have one. You will work better after a break anyway.

Another thing about over-posting is that it can overwhelm people. When people unsubscribe from an RSS feed or a social media account it is usually because of over-posting. Readers may also miss a post if you overload them. So where is the sweet spot?

The more you post the more traffic you can get via search engines, RSS feeds and social media. You may upset some readers but will gain others. Some topics will have more to write about than others. Even when I have been busy I have made sure that there are daily updates on Frost. I post at least once a day and I have found at least three posts and as much as ten a day works. I don't tend to post on weekends though. This is because I am trying to cure my workaholism and have decided to try and take weekends off. I only occasionally break this. Not all of the posts will get a lot of hits but the more content you have, the more readers you are likely to engage. If you look at the very popular blogs you will see that they tend to post frequently but their posts tend to be shorter.

Keeping up the momentum by posting at least once daily is a good idea. This keeps readers coming back because they know there will be something to read and it also helps your SEO because search engines will know that your site is updated daily. Posting at the same time every day can also help with reader engagement. If someone follows your blog on social media then they actively want you to communicate with them, by doing so you are only giving them what they want.

Your post frequency is an experiment but eventually you will find out what works for you and also for your readers. Do frequent market research on your blog and don't be scared to ask your readers what they want. As time goes by and you earn some money it is possible that you could pay people to help run your blog but until then try and think what is best for you and your readers. You don't want to burn out or run out of things to say. As you are starting out (if you are) try and post four to five times a week. This starts you into a rhythm and will start to get you readers.

If you are still unsure then look at your favourite blogs and look at how often they post articles. Think about how you feel about that? Do you want more or less? Always look at blogging as a business.

CATEGORIES

Make sure you have categories in your blog. This helps your site get indexed by search engines when they scan your site but also helps readers find the post in the topic that they are interested in. Category pages should be updated as frequently as you can, so if you find that you are not blogging regularly about a certain topic then get rid of that category page.

Types of blog post to write: instructional, informative, profiles, interviews, case studies, reviews, lists, rants, comparison pieces, articles about other articles, problem solving, research pieces (surveys, statistics, charts) , inspirational pieces, critiques (be respectful, insightful and only offer constructive criticism, not an outright attack), debate, prediction or yearly round-ups, collation posts, what-if posts (hypothetical) , satire (note that some people will take it seriously and react strongly.

Try to explain that it is not real to them very gently), parody, humour, memes, projects, competitions, quizzes, awards, polls.

Posts that cause your readers to interact are always good. Comments give your blog authority and it will make your readers also feel like they are part of a community.

Instructional posts are not only popular but can get hits even years later. Especially if your post gets on the front page of a search engine. People constantly search online for how to solve their problems, if you can solve these in a post then you have post gold.

As you continue to be a writer you will find that inspiration will come to you. You will find it easier to come up with ideas and will see topics and news items that will get a lot of hits. The more you are an editor and writer of your own blog, the better you will become at finding good content and getting it out there. Most importantly: trust yourself.

Writing a series is also a good idea. I did a 30 day no-sugar diet and blogged about it every single day. This not only got hits on the post I wrote that day, but all of the others too. I included lots of facts and statistics on sugar and health in these posts and a year later people were still reading them and remembered that I wrote them. Set yourself a challenge and blog about it every day and you will attract readers and those who want to do the same but don't know how. People will keep reading to see how you get on. Title your series properly so people know the posts belong to each other. Announce the series in an introductory post, try to create a bit of a buzz and let people know what the challenge is and how long you will be doing it for. Also post about it on your social media channels. When doing a series always link to the other posts. Whether as a chain link (with the previous and next post linked in) or link to them all in the introductory post, and then include that link in all of the posts. This will help people who come to the series as time goes on. End the series well. Give it a clear, satisfying end point, summarising all of your points and reaching a conclusion.

The best series will be practical and teach your reader something. Respond to a need of the readers and you will have a winning blog series that will engage readers and get you plenty of hits.

If you have learned anything so far it is that a blogger's work is never done. It is not just a full time job, it is a business. A bottomless black hole you could invest every minute of your life into and it would still need something. Don't despair, however, just work smarter, not harder. Set yourself boundaries and keep your work/life balance in mind. Be careful not to burn yourself out as this does no one any favours.

Having a popular blog gives you a platform. That cannot be underestimated in today's society. It is a huge selling point.

Put time and effort into writing titles and it will pay off.

Encourage people to comment on your posts. Ask them questions. Invite them to comment and interact with people who comment.

Be controversial

When people start fighting ....make sure it is kept clean. Delete and block abuse and never allow trolling. Drawing boundaries. Boundaries are good. No racism, sexism or bullying makes sure your blog is a great place where people can comment and feel safe. Trolls ruin it for everyone. Block them.

Dealing with negative comments. Try to brush off negativity. You will get people who disagree with you and that is fine, but other people will be rude and mean. It is very easy to be rude and mean anonymously, behind a keyboard. Brush it off and remind yourself of the positive comments instead.

WRITING SEO FRIENDLY POSTS.

The amazing Moz blog, do a free beginners guide to SEO which you can find via this link: http://moz.com/beginners-guide-to-seo They refer to it as "The Beginners' Guide to Search Engine Optimization (SEO). This is an in-depth tutorial on how search engines work.. This guide covers the fundamental strategies that make websites search engine-friendly." You can even download a free copy. It has been read by over a million people. Read it and learn. They say "Sometimes SEO is simply a matter of making sure your site is structured in a way that search engines understand. and the majority of web traffic is driven by the major commercial search engines, Google, Bing, and Yahoo!."

Writing good content is all well and good, but people still need to be able to find it. It is not just about sharing it on social media.

- Consider using an SEO plug-in for your blog. Yoast is a good one.
- Update your blog regularly. Fresh content will have people coming back.
- Make sure the post is clear to read.

- Use headings. This makes the post easy to read and has the all-important keywords.

More Tips

- Content: be topical, read papers and choose a story to write about. Do a top tips post.

- End blog posts with a call to action. You can use any action, ask them to comment and give their opinion, ask them to sign up to your newsletter or follow you on one of your social media accounts. Don't leave your readers wondering what to do next, tell them.

- Have questions as titles; How, where, what, who, why. Any of these work. Answer any questions your readers might have.

- I don't always follow my own advice. This is human nature but re-read this book through your blogging your journey and incorporate the advice within it. I know I will.

- Remember: Use titles that attract visitors

Interview someone. You could interview someone in your industry, a fellow blogger, anyone who would be of interest to your readers, or a client or customer. You can do the interview in person, over the phone, over Skype or via email. I mostly do interviews by email as transcribing interviews takes a significant amount of time and is very boring.

Reasons businesses should guest post on blogs: more inbound links boost SEO, more visitors, more credibility, the posts will get indexed, free marketing, it builds trust and gives greater control of your brand.

When doing reviews for brands: do not give copy approval, do not be bullied and do not feel like you need to send them the review first. It is not a reasonable request.

Be more niche and targeted with your long tail keyword tags. A long tail keyword is when you tag a phrase or sentence rather than one word.

Never plagiarise, always be honest. Link to others. Admit mistakes and correct them quickly. Respect other people's privacy. Always respect the law. Disclose affiliates and sponsored posts.

Do a day in the life piece. These are great and tend to be popular.

Always make sure your blog has pictures. They must have pictures. In fact, make sure every post has a picture. This will make sure it gets pinned and is read and shared more widely.

Think targeted and niche, not generic and common when it comes to tags and keywords. Make sure every post has a picture. This will make sure it gets pinned and is read and shared

Set up a Google Alert for the key words that you use. This will let you know when your post has been indexed. To set up Google Alerts go to google.com/alerts. Sign in if you have a Google account, if you don't you will have to get one. Put in the keyword you want to track and then choose how often you want to be alerted: daily/weekly. You can get alerts straight to your inbox. Very handy.

Do a roundup of previous posts that have done well. You just need an introduction and a way to link the posts. 'Most popular' or 'Top Fashion posts'. Whatever works.

Use clicky stats to track blog posts. getclicky.com

Give your blog the personal touch. Write about any of the following: how you got where you are, any struggles you had to overcome and how you did so, how you got started, why you choose your specific career path.

Analyse magazines on the newsstands to see what titles jump out at you and make you want to read them. Take this knowledge and use it for your blog post titles.

Tag your posts. Four or five tags are good.

You could also include a tag cloud. The more you use a tag, the bigger it will be. People can click on that tag and the articles associated with that tag will appear.

When commenting on other people's blogs be helpful and constructive, leave your URL in the appropriate section. Don't be rude or aggressive or just comment for the sake of it. Use your own name, not the name of the blog and don't leave your URL in the body of the comment. Giving comments on other blogs gets comments on yours.

Use anchor text when linking. This means you don't just put 'here' or 'this link'. You would put 'cat video' if you were linking to a cat video or 'wedding planning' if you were linking to a wedding planning company. This is great for SEO. This is even better than the link being a company name or something generic.

A mixture of SEO and social media will build traffic.

Analyse your analytics and focus on the articles that are high quality and have high traffic. Learn from mistakes.

For film reviews and events contact film studios like Fox, Universal and Disney. Contact their regional offices.

Keep an eye on what the new thing is and drop things that are no longer relevant and outdated. Think of new ways to publish things.

CHAPTER 4: MEDIA. PICTURES AND VIDEO

You can get pictures from your blog from stock photo sites like Rex Features, Getty Images, Wireimage, iStockphoto.com and 123rf.com. All except the last two will probably be very expensive however. To get free pictures you can go to Google Images, enter what type of picture you want, 'blue flowers' for example, click on the button in the far right corner near the safe search option and click on the advanced search option, go to the bottom of the page and select free to use or share, even commercially: You now have free images you can use for your post. The same thing can be done on other search engines too.

The best thing to do is to take your own pictures and title them properly.

If you are going to be taking a lot of pictures for your blog then you should invest in a camera. I have a Canon 60D. It was expensive but worth every penny. You can also make cinema-quality video with it. Learn how to use the camera properly as there is no point in buying an expensive camera if you never learn how to use it. Learn about staging, composition and editing too. There is a great cinematographer called Phillip Bloom. A lot of it is video based but he still teaches you how to use the camera and do lighting. http://philipbloom.net

Look at print magazine to learn how to stage pictures. This is particularly useful for gift lists. Fashion magazines like Glamour and ELLE are great to look and learn from. One of the most important things about photography is lighting. If you can learn how to light pictures properly then they will be stunning and you will be a great photographer. When it comes to lighting you don't need professional lights. You can use a lamp, daylight or even a torch. Indirect daylight works best. Avoid using your flash. Just use your imagination.

Photography is also a skill you can turn into another way to make money. When it comes to cameras it is always better to spend money on the lens rather than the camera body. The camera body can last for a long time, but upgrading the lens if you have some money can make all of the difference. Don't panic, even if you invest in a camera you can take great pictures just learning the basics and even using manual mode.

I take pictures on my iPhone and iPad quite a lot and not only do they take great pictures and are incredibly convenient, you can also easily upload the photos to Instagram and put a nice filter on them. It is easy to share pictures this way too. Always check the background of your pictures. Make sure the background is plain and not distracting. It may be worth doing a photography course. Either online or in person. You don't need to do an expensive one, just one that at least teaches you the basics and lighting and composition. If you don't want to take your own pictures, use stock photos.

Don't use blurry pictures. Make sure they are sharp and in focus. They must always look professional. Pictures taken in daylight are best. Get as close to the subject as possible. It will make your pictures look more professional. Cameras in phones are so good today it is quite easy to take great pictures. Use the image size which works best for your site. This will differ for different sites. Look at your site objectively or ask a friend. Keep in mind that pictures that are too big will affect loading time and will put some readers off.

Never steal pictures.

There is free picture and video editing software out there. Like Photobucket and PicMonkey.

Show article snippets on your homepage with a featured image instead of full length articles. This will keep your blog looking tidier and get you more page views. It also looks better.

If you want stock pictures you can buy them from agencies like wireimage.com, gettyimages.com and rexfeatures.com. It will cost you about £60 to use one image online!. You will need to sign up to each of these agencies to access their pictures. £60 is a lot of money, however, especially when you are just starting out. It's much better to take your own pictures or free pictures in directories like istockphoto.com, everystockphoto.com, http://search.creativecommons.org and imagecollect.com. Remember you can get free pictures from PR companies.

If you do want to buy some pictures, negotiate with the agencies as it should be cheaper to buy a picture for a blog than for a newspaper or magazine. Image Collect (imagecollect.com) allows you to download a certain number of pictures every month for $99. This can work out a lot cheaper than other options. You could probably get 15 pictures for less than the price of one. iStockphoto also allows you to sell your images. You get between 15-40 per cent of the sale price.

Wikimedia Commons has a lot of great pictures which are in the public domain. Go to commons.wikimedia.org. flickr.com also tend to have some good images. Use their advanced search option to make sure you use a picture with the proper license. As does morguefile.com, everystockphoto.com. Everystockphoto.com allows you to search different photo-websites and filter your results to the license you need.

When it comes to images remember: always check the license. There are other free licence options. Just always check and make sure the image is free to use. It is always nice to credit images if you can.

A creative commons licence tends to have limitations on it but you can still use them as long as you credit the source. There may be other limitations so always check. Make sure any pictures you use have a public domain licence with no limitations. Otherwise you could get sued and end up thousands of pounds out of pocket. Never mind the fact it is illegal to steal someone else's intellectual property.

USE PHOTO-EDITING SOFTWARE TO MAKE YOUR PICTURES LOOK BETTER

iPhoto: comes free with Macs. I use it and love it. Easy to use and free.

Instagram: great not only for networking and looking at beautiful pictures. It has a number of digital filters that can look amazing. I love it. Download the app for your iPhone if you have one. And your iPad. It also has tens of millions of users who are all possible readers of your blog.

Give variety with your pictures. Have some close-ups, pictures of you and other writers, panoramic … make your pictures good and you really will improve your blog and gain new readers.

Create collages using picmonkey.com or polyvore.com

Look through magazines to see how they use pictures. Steal their ideas liberally.

Another great idea is to use photo galleries. Not only do people love them, but they all add to your page views. Ever go to a site and then see a photo gallery where the pictures are in a slideshow? This is incredibly smart as each new picture counts as a page view, upping the page views of your blog and making you more attractive to advertisers. This also increases the amount of time spent on your site. You can create slideshows with Flickr or use a blog plugin. WordPress have a Next Gen gallery plugin.

OTHER EDITING PROGRAMS

Adobe Photoshop: expensive but advanced. Adobe Photoshop Elements is cheaper and should suffice if you won't be doing lots of fancy editing. The price difference is about £500.

Picasa: free to use. picasa.google.com is easy to download from Google. This free software is easy to use and quick. Picasa is also integrated with Google + and you can then share your picture on Google + with one button. Old pictures, edited and original, are saved in a folder.

PicMonkey: If you don't want to download any software then PicMonkey is for you. It is free and you just upload your picture and then edit it online.

Make sure the picture suits the story. It should have a similar tone. Big pictures are great and so are many at intervals throughout the text. Try to evoke an emotion for that particular article. You don't have to be obvious when choosing pictures. You can do something that suggests something rather than something in-your-face. Your picture should encapsulate the core statement of your article or at least show some insight to it. You can choose pictures that are a metaphor for your article, rather than a direct link.

Humorous pictures are great.

Use natural light for food photography. In fact, natural daylight is best for photography generally.

VIDEO.

You don't need to do videos on your blog but they can add a new dimension. YouTube is also great for vlogging (video blogging) and many bloggers make a lot of money from making videos. There is more information on YouTube in the social media chapter. Don't just post a video for the sake of it. Every one should reflect your brand. Always think quality over quantity. Make sure videos are well-shot. No shaky camera work (use a tripod if you can or steady your elbows against your body or a flat surface) and take lighting into consideration. Natural light is best. Look on YouTube for videos on lighting.

Video should have a purpose. Even if that purpose is merely to entertain. Sound is very important when it comes to video. Always make sure the sound is the best it can be. It will help to use a separate microphone. Audacity is a great site that lets you edit sound for free. If it is not, reshoot or dub over it. In the past I have used a Flip Camera and a Panasonic camera which are tiny, look just like phones and have USB keys that flip out from the camera, letting you upload the footage straight to YouTube. Very handy indeed. YouTube also allows you to edit your videos. The options are good and you can even cut and edit, fix the sound and stabilise the image.

I have a Canon 60D which I love. It was very expensive. Over £800 but it was worth it. It shoots video which is so good it is cinema-quality. If you buy a camera make sure it has the capability to plug an external microphone in. As I said, sound is important and the investment of an external microphone will make a huge difference to the quality of your video. Make sure your camera films in HD (High definition).

When shooting, always make sure the battery is fully charged and you have a spare. Also check that you have enough space on your SD card and a spare one too.

It is also wise to invest in a tripod. I once bought a pretty good tripod for a mobile phone from the pound store. Look online and always read reviews. Shaky footage is never good and no one will watch your videos if they make them feel nauseous. YouTube allow you to edit videos when you upload them on to the site. This includes shakiness. If you are filming on your phone then try to keep your hand as steady as possible. It is also good to try to lean on something. Or hold your elbow with the other hand and lean against the body. You will pick up little tricks along the way. When it comes to filming, check the background. Make sure there is nothing too distracting or off-putting. Check your sound levels too.

Video is time-consuming and can be hard to make so make sure it is worth it for you. Remember a five minute video is still only one page view.

Vine

You can film on your phone or tablet and upload your videos straight to Vine. Vine allows video that is a few minutes long and is a popular platform to share video on. You can download the app straight to your phone.

Editing your video.

You can use the free video-editing software on your computer. It should be good enough to make videos for your blog. With Windows this would be Windows Movie Maker and with a Mac, iMovie. I use iMovie and I think it is good and easy to use.

Professional software you can use includes Adobe Premiere Pro (or the cheaper version, Adobe Premiere Elements) or Final Cut Pro (the cheaper version of this is Final Cut Express). Editing video is harder than it looks. After you have tried it a few times it won't be so scary and you will be able to make good videos. You also don't have to spend any money unless you decide to make a feature film, the free stuff works just as well. There is also a lot of good help on YouTube that teaches you to edit.

When it comes to editing videos it will be helpful to learn how to do the following things:

Adding credits and titles. Also include a watermark of your site so people know where the video came from and you get credited if anyone else uses it. Trim the clips, add still images, apply transitions (this looks much better and more professional than something just finishing). You can also use music to make your video better. Do not use music you do not own the rights to however. Make sure anything you use is licensed for commercial use. You can get free music here: http://www.bensound.com or put 'licence-free music' into Google.

Uploading a video to your blog can be hard and also use a lot of gigabytes. It is much easier to upload it to Vimeo or YouTube and then embed it on your site. Make sure your blog has its own YouTube channel. If it gets a lot of hits you can even become a YouTube Partner and then make a lot of money. Vimeo has millions of users and YouTube has over 500 million users. Wow. People can even stumble onto your video by searching for something else. This will gain you more viewers and expand your brand. This opens you up to a new market and the more markets the better. You want to get your name out there as much as possible. You don't have to choose between Vimeo and YouTube, you can put your videos on both. The more channels you are on, the more you will get your brand out there. Make sure you tag your videos properly. This will make sure people find them. YouTube is also owned by Google so tagging your videos properly will get them ranked higher.

To embed the video on your site go to share and then click on embed. Copy the code and then paste it on your site. Easy. You can also change the size of the video. Encourage people to subscribe and comment on your videos. Do the same for them. The different sites have different audiences. Others you can try include Blip.TV, Metacafe and Yahoo Video.

More tips.

Make things good but don't get obsessed with perfection

It is always better to take the pictures yourself and tag them properly. You can get a surprising amount of traffic this way. A lot of my traffic comes from Google images. Alt tag (an ALT tag is HTML code which allows search engines to read and categorise pictures and video. There would be no words otherwise and people would not be able to find specific images. This is good for SEO) it properly. It is easy to do this on WordPress. Just put the keyword in the appropriate space.

Focus and have an identity.

Have a logo that clearly identifies your brand.

Keep giving people what they want.

CHAPTER 5: WORKING WITH PR PEOPLE

PR stands for public relations. Brands and people hire PR agencies to manage their image and get them good press. Most PR people are amazing; the ones that are good at their job are brilliant and to use a cliché, are worth their weight in gold. Building relationships with good PR people is an important part of building a blog. Through them you get invites, press releases and products to review. Try to build up your relationship with key PR people in your niche. Of course, you can run a successful blog without working with PR people, but they help you get in touch with brands and learn about the latest news and product launches.

While working with PR people is a gateway to great brands and events, don't get obsessed with working with PR people. Be creative and do your own thing. You will meet them as you attend events and launches; remember to hand out your business cards. Browse websites for a company's PR details. They might do it in-house or hire a PR firm.

Always ask the PR to send things in a format you can use. I hate PDFs, you can't lift the images nor do they copy and paste well. A Word document and a separate image is best. Ditto with sending a press release as an image. You can't copy and paste an image. Thank people. It will make them remember you. Tweet appreciation and if you can send links to the PR company do so. As you get busy you won't have time but always be nice and professional.

Not all PR people are wonderful. Here are some of my PR pet hates:

PRESS RELEASES

I get hundreds of press releases every day so could never reply to all of the people saying it is not for Frost, and to be perfectly honest: this would be a waste of my time. Most PR people do not expect a reply, they send press releases en-masse to a database but some will send it directly to you or at least put your name in. And then send you short emails about whether it is right for you and can you please reply. We rarely put a press release on Frost and don't take kindly to tetchy emails demanding replies. Don't feel guilty when the same happens to you. A press release is just a press release, not a personal message. Always value your time.

ASKING WHEN A REVIEW WILL BE UP

Asking when the review will be up and constantly harassing. This is especially annoying when you've been sent a beauty product. It takes months to see a change in your skin when using a beauty product but some PR people seem to think they can send you a product and have a review up in a week.

One PR person called my personal mobile phone to ask if I had gotten a press release they had just sent. I was not amused and certainly never used their release. My personal number was given to them for a courier who was dropping off a review product. The fact that they used it when they said they wouldn't broke my trust in them.

ASKING IF YOU GOT THEIR EMAIL

If you pressed 'send' I got your email.

ADDING A LINK

Can you please add a link? No, we can't. That makes it a sponsored post and you have already been given free publicity.

REMOVING A LINK

Can you please remove a link? No, we can't. Only advertisers who take out a clearly stated sponsored post get to make demands.

CAN YOU CHANGE THIS/ADD THIS

No. No one gets copy approval and the editor's decision is final. Funnily enough, it is always the least talented people who want copy approval or lots of changes. When I interviewed Zac Goldsmith and Alain De Botton neither of them asked for copy approval but I have had many people send me emails demanding lots of changes. My loyalty is to my reader and I don't work for them.

Politely refuse changes as it is not a free advertisement but your opinion. They would not do this to a big magazine or newspaper, don't let them do it to you. Some people don't give bloggers the same respect they give print publications. Don't tolerate it.

TIPS

- You don't have to work with PR people; it will depend on your blog.
- A good PR person is worth their weight in gold
- Remember that PR people need you, so don't let them be rude to you or treat you badly.
- Meet up with PR people so they can showcase their clients' products to you.
- Save time by skim reading press releases and don't reply to them.
- Always be professional and polite

PRESS EVENTS

Press events can be a lot of fun. There are usually lots of cool people, fun things, free drinks, canapés and entertainments Sometimes it feels like going to a party. You also get to test the latest products and speak to experts. If you are a beauty or tech blogger, going to a press event in that niche and getting to play with the latest products is a lot of fun indeed.

Some press events treat 'online' as second class citizens. Years ago when I was first starting out I went to a press event where the print media got a fabulous goodie bag as they were walking out and they asked me to wait so they could go and get mine. They came back with a canvas bag stuffed with a neon orange jumper and a pair of leopard print knickers in a size 16 (I am a size 8/10). Charming indeed. This happens quite a lot, getting either a lesser goodie bag or none at all. Of course we don't blog for goodie bags but being treated like a second-class citizen is no-one's idea of fun. I never return to these press events. If people treat you badly, move on. There are a ton of PR companies and press events to go to. Don't let anyone be mean to you.

PUBLICITY AND PR FOR YOUR BLOG

To get some publicity for your blog send email alerts to the media when you have a press release that might be of interest to them. This will make you legitimate and get you a lot of traffic. Tailor your press releases to each publication.

Working with a PR company will not be viable unless you make a lot of money as they are expensive. If you have the money find a PR company that works in your sector. Call them and ask for a quote. Ask what kind of coverage you will get for that.

Doing Your Own PR

Make a list of publications you want to be featured in. Always read a couple of issues of the magazine to get a feel for what they feature and also to make sure they have not published anything similar. Make a list of journalists, editors and writers you want to contact. Don't just contact anyone, be strategic. Contact magazines, broadcast media, blogs, sites and newspapers. Contact each publication you are interested in and ask for the name and contact details of the relevant person. The receptionist might not want to give the details but just ask for the name and email address of the person. You can also find this type of information in the Writer's and Artist's Yearbook and in Gorkana and the Diary Directory. A subscription to Gorkana is not cheap however so you might not be able to afford this, at least not right away. Gorkana has a database containing a lot of journalists' details. If it is a print publication or a newspaper then buy a copy as the masthead will probably have the details of the person you need. Also try the contact page on their website. Be persistent and don't give up. Prove that you have done your research as this means you will be more likely to be successful and get read. A lot of people won't go to the effort so always go the extra mile.

Writing Your Own Press Releases

A press release should be around 500 words. It should contain all of the facts and be a concise summary. Be sure to include contact details. Make sure you have quotes ready in case the journalists ask for any. Choose the thing that is most interesting on your blog and lead with that. Put forward your best content. Be relevant. If you cannot think of something then lead with something seasonal or with a theme. Magazines work about three months in advance, sometimes more. Think Valentine's Day, Christmas, New Year resolutions and things like that.

For more information on writing a press release: pressreleasewriting.com/10_essential_tips.htm, publicity insider.com/release.asp or wikihow.com/write-a-press-release

Always follow up with a phone call and take this opportunity to ask the journalist what they cover and, if it is not right for them, what type of thing would be. The phone call also lets you build up a relationship with that journalist. As in any business, good relationships are key.

If this all sound like too much effort, or you want to reach a lot of people, you can use a service like PRNewswire or Gorkana who both do a press release distribution service. This costs money however so check out their rates to make sure they are affordable. PRNewswire is US based while Gorkana is UK based.

Create content worth sharing. Each time someone shares your content you reach a new audience.

Chapter 6: Promoting and Marketing Your Blog.

Content may be king but that does not mean it will get read. The sad fact is, the best blog post you have written won't always be widely read. It can be devastating when this happens but you just have to get on with it. And when I say 'on with it' I mean promoting and marketing your blog. Do this while writing good content and sharing it can build your blog up slowly through word-of-mouth, this can be a slow process that could take years. So this chapter is on how to get readers and keep them.

A good way to build your blog is to have a number of posts that are not time-sensitive. News items tend to get read at the time and then people move on to the next story. Having a number of articles that are educational or instructional can not only get you many readers at the time, but also for years down the line. I have a number of posts on Frost Magazine that rank well in Google and constantly get hits. Reviews are also good as people want to read reviews and get other people's opinions on something before they buy. Recipes also work, as do 'how to' articles, interviews and profiles. Research what you think your readers might be interested in, and then give it to them. True life experience and opinion pieces can also get hits at the time and years down the line. I wrote a piece on my grandfather and dealing with his death, not only does it get hits years later, but people still send me emails and lovely comments saying how much it moved them or helped deal with a death in their own family. It makes it all worth it.

For these types of flagship articles the following are all good ideas: resources, reference, tutorials, tips, advice, lists, reviews, recipes. The key is to create compelling content that not only gets people reading, but keeps them coming back.

Make sure you keep updating your blog and show the audience that if they subscribe or bookmark your blog then they will find something great the next time they visit. You don't have to update your blog every day long-term, but when you are starting out try and keep the momentum up. You want to draw people in and turn them into loyal readers.

When reading other blogs and publications think about the articles you read. Why did you read them? How did they draw you in? Analyse everything and then apply it to your blog.

Another way to get readers it to comment on other blogs. Comment on blogs that are similar to yours. Most of these comments boards allow a link to your blog when you comment. Provide something valuable to say and you will get your brand known by the right people. Do not spam however, if links are not normally put by people, and you don't have anything relevant to say then you will just upset people and become known for spamming. Never a good thing. Reputation is everything. Build up relationships instead.

When it comes to other blogs and publications, be generous with your links. The blog you link to might link back and you could even build a relationship with them. WordPress also does a thing called 'trackback' where you get a notification that someone has linked to you and commented about an article that you wrote. You can then approve this trackback and the link to that post will be in your comments section underneath your post. Watch out for spam however. Only approve something if you know it is genuine. Trackbacks also work the other way, your blog link will appear in that blog's comments section if you link to them. This is good for SEO and marketing.

Linking to another blog might not get you anything immediately but could build up a relationship longer-term.

HERE ARE SOME OTHER TYPES OF ARTICLES AND IDEAS THAT CAN GET YOUR BLOG LOTS OF HITS

- Doing surveys and then releasing the results to the general media. The media love surveys and statistics and this could get you wide-spread PR in lots of mainstream publications.
- Lists - people love them. List the Top 10 of something.
- Have a scoop. This is old school but if you can get a scoop not only will it get you hits, but a good scoop will also be picked up by other publications and could even make it into the mainstream media. This type of publicity for your blog is priceless.
- Resources: creating useful resources for people in your expertise won't only get you hits immediately but will also get hits long term.
- Competitions. People love free stuff. Every time I run a competition on Frost it gets a lot of hits and I also get people signing up to our various social media accounts and subscribing. Competitions are great for getting new readers and also for making those readers stick around for a while to see if they won. Of course, the flip side is that some people will end up disappointed as not everyone can be a winner. Make the competition easy to enter. You should be able to get a brand to supply you with competition prize, put a media alert out on Gorkana. If you are starting out then use something you have gotten in a goodie bag or buy something to give away yourself. The investment should recoup itself. In fact, we did this when Frost was a fledgling, giving away some beauty products we got in a goodie bag to a lucky winner. To recoup your money you could also choose a prize which you can promote via one of your affiliate links. Always have an end date for competitions. Readers don't want

them to run on forever but you also want to give time for word-of-mouth to build and give people enough time to enter. A month is a good length. I also find that when I do competitions people tend to put the link to the competition on various forums, not only gaining me new readers, but also links. All good stuff.

- Interviews: interviewing famous people, or those successful in their profession can bring in lots of hits and also prestige at getting a 'name' for your blog.

- Awards. Doing an award can pay off massively. Think of the print publications GQ and Glamour. They both have awards and this gives them prestige and bundles of publicity. There is no reason why you cannot do the same, even if you do it in a much smaller way. Think of a beauty award or a separate awards in your blog niche.

- Freebies: people love free stuff. They really do. Offer something of value and you are on to a winner.

- Tools. Create a cool tool which advances people's lives. A while ago there was a blogger who made a tool which allowed women to put in their measurements and find out what dress size they were in each store. Not only was this hugely popular, but it was also covered in all of the print women's magazines.

- Quizzes. People also love quizzes, personality tests and surveys in general. You have probably seen these types of things on Facebook and such.

The best posts don't age and get hits continuously over time. Next time you read something and it really draws you in, or you bookmark an article, think about why you did it and what you could do to make your own posts even better.

Another way to get great ideas and to find out what works and what doesn't is to check our social bookmarking sites like Reddit, StumbleUpon, Bloglovin' and Digg to see what is popular and what works and doesn't. What headlines grab you and what ones don't make you click.

Which brings us to

SOCIAL BOOKMARKING SITES.

It is very easy to become obsessed with social bookmarking sites. Having an article voted up on one of these sites means an article going viral and thousands or millions of readers flocking to your blog. Sites like reddit.com, StumbleUpon, digg.com and del.icio.us can make your blog, gaining you lots of readers, if only temporary. I find that different social bookmarking sites work for different people. Some I get a lot of hits from, others barely anything.

These sites work by submitting your article (or someone else doing so) and then it being voted up or down by the members of that site. If you get a lot of votes, you get a lot of hits. Create accounts on all of the different bookmarking sites, initially at least. You can always drop the ones that don't work for you later on if you don't have time to use them. Also make sure that you have a plugin on your site that makes social sharing easy. Make sure it has sharing buttons for the following: Pinterest, Google +, Reddit, StumbleUpon, Digg, Twitter, Facebook and LinkedIn. A button that allows readers to email the article to other people is also useful. This makes sure that people can share your post easily and gives it a better chance of going viral. Sites which do not make it easy for readers to share their content do themselves a huge disservice. Why write good content and then not give people the tools to share it?

Pinterest is a site where people pin pictures to boards. People can then share, like and comment on the pictures. The good thing about sharing on Pinterest is that each of your pictures is linked to your site. I know blogs whose major source of incoming traffic is pictures shared on Pinterest. This works if you have a picture-heavy blog, but also when you share one picture from an interesting post and tag it properly.

I find Reddit is very good for incoming traffic. It can be hard to know which interest to put an article under however. There is a lot of choice and choosing the correct one can make all of the difference.

It may be worth your while to go through Digg, StumbleUpon and Reddit to see what works and what doesn't. This may not be the best strategy and may not be worth your time but it is one way to do it. Think about what is popular and gets a lot of hits and votes and what doesn't. Research will always give your business the edge.

Networking is vital.

Join blogging groups on Facebook and Twitter. Join forums. Join blogging communities in your niche and then network actively within them.

Put the subscribe button somewhere prominent on your blog and make it easy to do so. Make sure it works. You can easily add a widget in the sidebar for people to subscribe. Do competitions on your blog and make subscribing to the site a criteria for winning. This helps to build your email list of subscribers. Something that is very valuable.

Add a signature to the bottom of your email with a link to your blog. Also add your blog link to your Facebook, Twitter, LinkedIn, Instagram and any other websites you have or social media sites you are on. Get the word out there.

Write a mission statement for your blog. Be able to sum it up in one sentence. Keep editorial standards high and be consistent. Be proactive.

Sending out a newsletter reminds people that you exist and gives them a run-down of your best posts of that week or month. It is important to keep in people's minds. You can send newsletters with MailChimp, Vertical Response or Constant Contact. I use MailChimp which is popular and very easy to use. After you sign up you just use a template and drop and drag your content in. It looks great too. I put a picture in, the title and link the title to the article. Easy and simple. Remind people about your newsletter and ask them to sign up occasionally.

GETTING LINKS TO YOUR BLOG VIA GUEST POSTING.

I used to work for an SEO company and the main part of my job was to write guest posts which would be ghost-written by me with a link to the clients website. The irony is that in my other job, as editor and owner of Frost Media, I really hated receiving these types of emails because they were from businesses who could pay for a sponsored post but were trying to get a free link on my site by trying to procure a guest post instead. I hated the job and did not do it for long. People don't respect bloggers enough.

This does not mean that you should never take, nor do a guest post. Actual bloggers, especially when starting out, rarely have money. Writing a good guest post for a fellow blogger is a great way to get your name out there and build up a fan base. If people like your post they will click on the link to your site, and even if they don't it is great for your SEO. The blog you write for gets something out of it too in the shape of free content. Win win for both.

A great blog to guest post for is The Huffington Post. Find the editorial details of your edition (UK, US etc.) and then pitch them an article you have written. You never know, they may take you on as a writer.

Make a list of other blogs and publications that reach the type of readers that you want to reach. Or that have a lot of readers and authority. I almost fainted with joy when I noticed The Guardian had linked to Frost Magazine. I didn't send them a guest post or anything, they just liked an article I had written and linked to it. We got a lot of traffic from it. Have an email template which you can tweak to each publication. Be honest with them, don't say you are a huge fan and have read their blog for years if you haven't. Be genuine. Say you like their blog and that you would like to write an article for it on the condition that there is a link back to your site. The article is free but the link is your payment as a professional writer. Keep the email brief and do not just ask for a link. Links are worth something, offer them something in return. View it as a business transaction. Be professional and polite. You could also offer to link back to their site. A link for a link deal is a win for both parties.

WHO DO YOU KNOW? USE YOUR CONTACTS.

HOSTING EVENTS.

I did a launch party for Frost Magazine in 2010. It was very stressful and a lot of work, especially as the venue pulled out not long before the event and I had to find another one sharpish. However this gave us good publicity and started us off with a bang. It got good coverage and made us look professional. Get banners and posters with your logo and put them everywhere. Invite staff, PR people, and celebrities. Invite the media to cover your events as this will result in great publicity. Make sure everyone has a good time. Good planning is essential. Take the guest list seriously. Invite the editors of all of the major publications, and the small ones. Invite key players in your industry and invite important PR people. Parties are very expensive; make sure people deserve their space. It is harsh, but it's business.

Approach a hotel and ask them for a room you can use in exchange for bringing in new customers. To get people to come you have to play them off each other. Tell the celebrities the media is coming and then tell the media the same thing about the celebrities. Once you have celebrities and journalists attending you can contact alcohol brands. They should be up for providing some free alcohol in exchange for free publicity. Pitch to about ten different alcohol brands. Everyone likes to be written about. Play to their egos.

At your event always be on the ball. Do not drink. Distribute and collect business cards, work the room and try to talk to everyone, make everyone feel special.

Make sure you have a photographer and even a videographer. The photographer we hired for Frost Magazine was terrible and we ended up not even getting the pictures! So watch out and make sure you ask for good recommendations. A friend who can do the job well is a good idea if you cannot hire a professional. The people who attend the party will also want to know if they made it into a picture. Publish them all on your blog afterwards. A gallery would be best rather than a long post with tons of pictures.

Give guests a goodie bag. These don't have to cost you a lot of money. Ask brands if they want to supply something. Ask the alcohol brand if they have miniature bottles you can put in the bag. The bags you can buy cheaply from a supplier. Ask the PR people and the celebrities if they have anything they want to promote in return for the free publicity. Most will have something they want to promote and it will be cheaper to supply goods for a goodie bag than pay for proper advertising. Send everyone a thank you afterwards, hopefully with a link to the event press you have written.

Send a press release about the event, along with some pictures, to relevant publications. You never know who will feature it. Also send a press release to local media; they will be more likely to feature. After you send the press release call the news editor of each publication and tell them about your event and how amazing it was. Be enthusiastic and they might feature it. If you get your blog in the mainstream press then you will get a lot of traffic and hopefully some new readers.

Work with good people and cut the negative ones out. There is an old saying that you should judge someone by their friends. Truth is, people do judge people by the people they associate with. Make sure those people are good, decent, hardworking and professional.

Tell bloggers that you have linked to them. Text based links inside posts link higher than links on a blogroll.

Use keywords that are relevant to your blog over and over again.

Register your site with the search engines. They need to know you exist. Do this for Yahoo (siteexplorer.search.yahoo.com/submit), MSN Live Search (search.msn.com/docs/submit.aspx) and Google (google.com/addurl)

Advertise on Google AdSense. There is no minimum spend on Google AdSense. You pay for the clicks to your site, not the impressions. You get value. You can start whenever you want and have ads up the same day. You can also cancel at any time. Google provides a ranking tool which allows you to monitor the success of your campaign. This lets you make changes and analyse what is going well and what needs worked on. You do need credit in your account when you sign up to Google ads so you will need to pay a deposit via PayPal or your bank account. (google.com/adwords) Make sure you use the right keywords. The best ad will have a low Cost Per Click link (CPC) and a high Click Through Rate (CTR). This makes it financially worthwhile. Tweak your keywords until you get there.

When searching for keywords with Ad words you have a few options. You can choose 'exact match' and get shown the number of estimate searches for that exact search, use 'broad match' and 'similar' and related words will be included, and 'phrase match' will give you phrases included in your word/words search only.

Go to Search Engine Watch for tips. searchenginewatch.com

MERCHANDISE.

Zazzle, Vistaprint and Moo are places that you can buy merchandise from. They all have good rates. After you have your merchandise go somewhere where your readers hang out and hand out the merchandise. Be picky about who you give it to. It costs you money after all. Go to workshops, classes and places where your reader hangs out and network with them. Then hand out your merchandise. Don't act like a saleswomen or make people uncomfortable. Just hand it over after having a chat with a smile. Don't force it on people. When it comes to merchandise, a pen will always keep you in someone's mind.

BLOGGING NETWORKS.

Blogging Networks can be a great thing. I am with Handpicked Media. Blog networks are basically a collective of blogs all under one umbrella. The network you are with is basically a marketing agency, they do your advertising, give you support and promote you.

Some blog networks are huge, like Gawker Media and Weblogs, Inc. which was sold to AOL for an estimated $25 million in 2005. Needless to say, after that many more blog networks started up.

Things to look out for when joining a blog network:

- Revenue split. What is their cut?
- Support. How much will there be?
- Networking. Do they have the right contacts? Will they share them?
- Reputation. Do they have a good reputation?
- Contacts. Again, contacts are important. Make sure they have the right ones.

BLOG OWNERSHIP AND RIGHTS.

When I joined Handpicked Media after I had run Frost Magazine for a few years, I owned and still own, 100% of it. It is worth making sure that if you join another blog network that you retain the rights to your blog and your work. Some blog networks will want ownership of your blog and some will want to co-own it. Be very careful about this, if you leave will you be paid for what you did for the blog while you were there? Ask the following questions:

Who owns the URL and the blog? Who owns the content? What happens if I leave?

Also make sure you read every contract with a fine-tooth comb before signing anything. Seek legal advice if you think that you have to. It will save you money in the long run.

Your responsibilities: Be professional and always do what you are asked to a high standard.

To be in Handpicked Media you need to get a certain amount of unique users every month. Other blog networks will have their own rules and regulations. Many blog networks keep an eye out for talent and you might get invited to join one. If not then do your research and find out which blog network is for you. Go to their website and see if there is a page with the information on how to join. Follow the instructions very carefully and really sell yourself.

Put your blog on these directories: http://www.thelinkmedic.com/2010/09/over-25-great-sites-to-submit-your-blog.html

Before joining a blog network ask around and find out what experiences other people have had with them. Check out the blogs in their network and see how they are doing. Do you fit into their network? It can be nice to be part of a community and have support but make sure you join the right blog network for you.

Cross-promote with the other blogs in the network.

You could always start your own blog network. This won't be easy but you can do it.

CHAPTER 7: SEO AND OTHER GROWTH STRATEGY

SEO: INBOUND LINKS.

Every person who links to your site is a vote of approval for your site according to search engines. Each person who links to your site helps its SEO. Try and get links from highly valued sites. The best way to get links is to write content of value.

Add your blog to web directories.

Offer a link for a link.

You can also buy links. These are known as sponsored posts. I would not recommend a blogger doing this. Mostly because it takes quite a long time to make decent money blogging.

SEO: KEYWORDS.

Another good way to give your content the best chance of being read is to use keywords effectively. Think of the words people would put into a search engine to find your article and then use them within the article, repeated a number of times throughout.

You can add keywords to an article in the following ways: in the title, throughout the text in the post (best used near the beginning), image alt tags, bold text, heading and sub heading tags, links and in the URL.

Do not go overboard with keywords at the expense of your article. You want it to be readable and to flow. Don't ruin the reader experience for the sake of keywords. Use your own judgement and always think about your reader. Always be user-friendly and make sure your article does not look like spam.

Link to other articles on your blog to promote them and make sure you tag your article correctly and use good keywords in the anchor text.

Add a plugin that allows you to add metadescriptions (a snippet of what the article is about). Google ranks these higher than ordinary keyword tags.

Connect web profiles and also connect them to your blog. Tie everything back to your blog. Include your blog link in profiles. Have a watermark on pictures and your blogs URL on video and descriptions.

Use Google's rel+ author. You will get a profile picture next to all of your content. Good for branding and more clicks.

Find out what sites are linking to other sites in your niche and get some for yourself too. Conduct competitive link research to find out which of their posts are popular too. Also check out their marketing strategies. Research these for finding out what strategies work. Look for patterns. This is also good for finding guest blogging opportunities and general outreach.

Try and build up your technical knowledge so that if your blog breaks you can fix it yourself.

StumbleUpon. You can use their su.pr URL shortener. It adds the StumbleUpon button at the top, making it easy for people to share and rate your page or article. StumbleUpon will then send extra traffic to your site as a thank you for using their system. StumbleUpon also offer other tools for publishers. Check those out too.

SEO: Keywords you use in your post and links to and from your site.

Apparently there is a general rule that longer articles with 1-2% keyword inclusion produce better search results. Your subject keyword should be included 4-8 times for a 400 word article. With images use the 'alt+' attributes to describe the content in the image. This helps search engines understand what your post is about.

Have a relevant posts section underneath your post. You can use a plugin for this.

Another thing to avoid is duplicate content. Not just on your site but also on other sites. Google warns against duplicate content in its guidelines and penalises sites which have duplicate content. This is because spammers put the same content on many sites and also steal content from other sites.

A great tool to use is the Google Webmaster Tools. Using the webmaster tools you can check to see if your site has any problems that are stopping it being indexed properly. This tool also allows you to see what phrases your site is ranked for.

It is not just about getting readers; it is also about keeping them and getting them to read more than one page. Here are some ways to do so:

Have a list of relevant posts below your article, link to your other posts within your posts,

Write a series and make sure you have category sections in your blog and highlight them.

You could even put a link to the category along the lines of 'read more posts like this in our wedding section'.

You could also do a list of your top 20 posts, or even your top 20 posts on certain subjects. This will allow new and old readers alike to read more of your great content.

Use 'Best of' lists to highlight your top and most-read articles.

On your homepage you can have the full blog post or excerpts. For Frost Magazine we have excerpts of the most recent posts along with a sliding bar. This means that readers have to click on the post to read the full article. Some people prefer to have the full posts on their homepage to make things easier for the reader but I have never had a problem with using excerpts and like to browse through the different posts that are of interest.

Have a brand page for LinkedIn, Google + and Facebook. Fill out the profiles as much as possible, have good pictures, compelling descriptions and update them. Research shows that the more description an account has, the higher engagement it has.

Forums. Engage in forums that are relevant to your blog. I once put a relevant link on a thread on a fashion forum I had used for years and been loyal to, only to get a very rude and bitchy email telling me to 'not come here and promote your own blog'. I had supported this site for years but after that I deleted my account and have never been back. Manners and courtesy cost nothing. Find friendly forums that are worth your time and allow people to share good, relevant posts.

ENCOURAGING COMMENTS.

Most readers will not comment on your posts but it pays to try and actively get some comments. Do this by asking readers what they think or by asking questions in your post or title, be controversial or inspire debate, always interact with the people who comment. As your blog grows you may not be able to reply to everyone but always make as much effort as you can. Be polite and professional when replying, no matter how rude someone is. When it comes to trolls, it is always best to just ignore them. They want you to react or get upset so don't give them the satisfaction. If someone points out something you have gotten wrong, a fact or a spelling or grammar error, then just be gracious and admit you got it wrong. It can be hard to not act defensively but the more gracious you are the better you come across and the more likely other people will feel secure enough to comment. I do admit that it is very annoying when you write a 700 word article and all someone can do is point out the one small grammar mistake in it. Don't take it to heart though, just be polite and thank them for pointing it out so you can correct it. Lastly, make it as easy to comment as possible. Not everyone will know how to. It will also put people off if they have to login or give their personal information to comment. Keep everything simple and user-friendly

Always think of ways to keep your readers interested. Analyse what is working and what is not. Think about what makes you continue to read certain blogs. What draws you in? Reader engagement is important; you want people staying on your site for as long as possible. To build a great blog you have to keep writing good content and let people know about it.

Another possible way to get more traffic is to have your posts translated into a different language. This may not be worth it but could be a way to gain more traffic.

Be different, find a gap and fill it. Have a unique take. Have staying power.

Always keep abreast of the industry. Follow the latest technology, sites and news. Keeping up with your industry always gives you the advantage. Research, experiment, encourage discussion and test out new things.

Stay positive.

Build awareness, credibility and revenue.

Make your site indispensable. If you can make your site the go-to site for your niche then not only will readers flock to your site for the latest news, but so will journalists and PR people. The more people who go to you for the latest news and exclusives, the more likely you are to get the top stories.

Breaking news is a good way to get readers. Be first and post it fast. Network with all of the big names in your industry. News can be hard to blog about because you need to post a constant stream of the latest news. Your content will also be dispensable. If you are doing all your own posting you may burn out or just not be able to keep up. You could start your blog with someone else or rope friends in. If you are doing a news blog then make sure you add something new. Don't just rewrite the same old dross. Add your opinion or write about it in a way that helps your reader understand it better. Add something to the story. Provide some background history to the story or give a prediction on what might happen. Either way: give it a unique spin.

To reiterate, here are some top blogging tips.

- As your blog grows reevaluate your worth. Always know your worth and don't be scared to ask for more money from advertisers.
- Put your audience first, be original, cover new ground. Be compelling, unique, useful and remarkable.
- Be well connected. It is not just about writing content. Network and meet the right people.
- Link to good, interesting stories.
- Post little and often.
- Tell a story and what you learned from it.
- Avoid over posting. You will drown your content and overwhelm readers.
- Have strong opinions.
- Be inclusive.

Consider putting your money back into the blog to grow it. You have to spend money to make money. Do your research and find out what works.

Use mixed media: video, audio, pictures, and then see what your readers respond to. Drop what doesn't work and keep what does.

How people make money differs from person to person. Some focus on advertising, some sell their products or services, others write books and some find affiliates are where it is at. Find the right path for you and follow it. There is no 'right' way to do it, only the right way for you.

Bob Dylan once sang that you need to serve somebody, and when you have a blog you do: the reader. Especially the loyal readers who stand by you. Nothing gives you a buzz like someone telling you how much they love your site and how often they read it. But after the buzz comes something else: pressure. Pressure to keep it up, pressure to keep people entertained. This is not necessarily a bad thing. Pressure is a privilege. I remember one reader telling me that she read Frost Magazine before going to bed each night. After she told me this, I had her in mind every time I wrote something or posted something from one of my writers. I didn't want to let her down. Constant, good content is what you readers deserve, and expect. To have readers and people who love your site is a huge deal, treat it with the respect it deserves. Take all feedback from your readers and use it. The good and the bad.

One of the best ways to give your audience what they want is to know who they are. Constantly research who your audience are and what is working for them. Through Google analytics, alexa.com and your Facebook page you should be able to find out the following: age, education level, gender and where they live. Always know who your readers are. Analyse what they love and hate. After you have done this start brainstorming for some content ideas that you think that they will love. Some will work and some won't: it is all a learning curve. Work on pushing your brand far and wide.

Tags

Add title tags (post title), meta descriptions and meta keywords to every post.

Title tag: Google only uses the first 70 characters. The title tag is the words in your browser window. The title tag is usually the post title but you can change it. The title tag is the most relevant and important on-site optimisation to Google. Always make sure you take the time to optimise your title tags. It is very important.

Meta descriptions: if you leave it blank, this will be the first 150 words of your post by default. This is what appears under the bold title in the Google search results.

Meta Keywords: Google does not put much importance into meta keywords but the other big search results like Yahoo and Bing do. These are the search keywords and phrases that you tag your post with.

Use a SEO plug-in if one does not come with your theme. Yoast has a lot of good feedback.

Long tail keywords. A long tail keyword is a number of keywords like 'very cute cat video' rather than just 'cute' or 'cat video.'

Google's goal is to give people the best result for their search term. Which doesn't mean that advertising with them won't help your cause. It always helps to be more specific. Target your tags to the audience.

The following things could get your site penalised: too much duplicate content, lots of short posts, and too many posts.

- Mix SEO with good content and you are on your way to a successful blog. Do what you can to optimise your posts and website pages.
- Do not get obsessed with SEO at the expense of everything else. Just write good content, do the best SEO you can, share on social media and make sure you have great pictures and web-design.
- Optimise every post and page on your site.
- Join online blogging groups and local meet-ups as well as conferences
- Some great blogging sites/groups: Independent Fashion Bloggers, FBL: Fashion, Beauty and Lifestyle Bloggers.

Google's job is to give people the most high quality and relevant search results. Google uses an algorithm to do this. Although Google's algorithm is a closely guarded secret which many SEO companies spend their time trying to game, a few things remain true. Keep these in mind when writing your blog post.

Use relevant keywords.

Google uses 'endorsements'. Links to your site and social media shares.

POPULARITY

Search engines value popularity. The more views a page gets, the higher its authority. It is the same thing with the domain, the more visitors, the higher the authority. You can use the Moz toolbar to find out your domain authority. The higher the better.

To boost your domain authority share your site more on social media, get more comments and write content that people won't be able to not share.

Links are the internet's endorsement. The more you get, the higher your authority and the higher your search ranking.

Guest posting is a great way to build links to your site. Link to your blog within the post or in your biography at the bottom.

It is a good thing to try to get some publicity in mainstream media. Newspapers and magazines have email addresses or forms for submitting news. Make sure you check all of the email addresses and send the email to the right person and address it to them personally. This will make it much more likely that your email will be read and you might get some publicity.

Reach out to people who curate content.

When it comes to keywords think about the intent of the relevant keyword searches. Are people researching, buying or browsing? 'How to' shows more intent to do the activity so people will be more likely to buy. Think about what the keyword indicates.

When it comes to keywords too little competition is not necessarily a good thing. It might mean that there is just no interest in that topic. Too much competition however may mean that you just get buried in amongst the vast amount of other content.

In the competition column Google Keyword Planner displays the competitiveness of each term. It also has a 'suggested bid' column which shows how much people will be willing to pay for clicks for that term. It makes sense that if people are willing to pay a lot of money then they will be getting something out of it.

Check out what Amazon is selling. Check your keywords on search engines too, this will let you know what your competition is and what is out there generally.

The key(!) to keywords is to use high volume, relevant keywords that have low competition. Use meta descriptions and title. Use relevant keywords as anchor text when doing guest posts. Also try to pick some sites that match your keyword.

.com .org and .net domains will rank higher than other domain endings and country specific domains, like co.uk, will rank higher in that specific country. Apparently domains with numbers are penalised and longer domains rank lower than those with short domains.

Google lets you claim authorship of your site. This is an important SEO strategy. This connects your site to your Google+ page. This will also mean that your site picture/logo will show up in search results next to your website. This is how to claim your site: http://plus.google.com/authorship

Google Page Rank shows how important a page's importance is. You can find out how to check your site's page rank here: https://support.google.com/toolbar/answer/79837?hl=en-GB

CHAPTER 8: SOCIAL MEDIA

Social media is important. Some blogs find that most of their traffic comes from Facebook or Twitter. While this is risky, you actually have certain sites who just focus on Facebook and have tens of millions of hits. The problem with this is that if Facebook change their algorithm then it can hurt your business and affect your traffic. Hopefully by this point you will have built up a loyal following anyway.

Try to have your traffic come from diverse sources.

Viral traffic can be the way to take your blog to the next level. The thing about viral growth is that you can't buy it, it only comes when you write an amazing blog post that people read and then share with others. It is basically word-of-mouth.

Hone your craft, write every single day, take great pictures and have a great blog design.

Learn how to capture viral traffic.

As you go on as editor and writer of your own blog, you will develop a skill for finding a story, writing it well and tailoring it to your audience. You will find you can find the stories, come up with the ideas that your readers love and keep coming back for. It is a wonderful feeling when this happens and is a valuable skill.

Social media options: Facebook, Twitter, Google+, Instagram, LinkedIn, StumbleUpon, Tumblr, YouTube, Reddit, Snapchat, Flickr, Vine, Pinterest...there are a lot and it can seem overwhelming. The key is to use all of them at first and then you will see which one works for you and your blog. Keep the ones that get you traffic and then forget the ones that just waste your precious time. Many of these sites link into each other. If you upload a picture to Instagram you can then share it on Facebook, Twitter, Tumblr and Flickr.

When it comes to social media always think about your ROI (Return on investment). If certain social media isn't working then let it go and work on the ones that are working well.

Know where your readers are.

Think about your reader demographic and where these people spend their time. For women aged 22-55 their most-used social media channel is Facebook and Pinterest. Do research on which social media channel your demographic uses so you can market your blog to the right audience.

Don't just focus on numbers either. If you get a lot of followers on one social media channel this does not mean as much as another one where you may have less but get more traffic through.

For Twitter, use hashtags.

Fake followers on Twitter are useless. Don't buy them and unfollow non-active accounts.

FACEBOOK

Also join groups on Facebook which are relevant and post on them too. Create your own groups too. Make sure your blog has a Facebook page that people can like. Share your posts on it (Word-Press can do this automatically) and also your personal page. Make sure posts shared on Face-book have a picture. They are much more likely to get shared and clicked on if so.

Run competitions to increase Facebook likes and engagement. Make it easy to like you on Face-book by having it on your blog's homepage. Remind people. Update your Facebook regularly. I use a WordPress plugin that automatically shares every single post that is published on Frost Maga-zine to our Facebook page. Use Facebook ads. Join pages which are similar to yours and com-ment and share on them. Just don't spam people or make a nuisance of yourself. Only post your content if it is relevant. Share your Facebook page on your other social media accounts. Promote your Facebook page on guest posts, have it on your business cards and add it to your email signa-ture.

FACEBOOK BUSINESS PAGES

Facebook changed its algorithm and a lot of people were upset and lost a lot of traffic. Many think this was a way to force businesses into paying for engagement through Facebooks ads. Some also grumble that they think the engagement from the paid ads is from fake accounts. Some peo-ple will incentivise likes, which is fine, but this may not mean engagement later on. The less en-gagement a Facebook page gets, the more Facebook will assume that no one is interested in it and will limit its reach. Really not fair but the harsh reality.

This is not to say that having thousands, or millions, of followers on a social media channel is a bad thing, it is not. It looks good for you and your business. It could even get you a book deal. So don't just think about quantity, but also quality. You want lots of followers but you also want them to be engaged.

- When it comes to Facebook have a long term strategy.
- Do regular posts and updates. Have a consistent schedule
- You can use Facebook's scheduling tool to schedule a number of posts a day. This will help with engagement.
- Focus on sharing your own content numerous times a day. Have gaps in-between if you can.
- Alternate between link posts and picture posts with the link in the description. Facebook pulls a picture from your link posts but it is not always the one that works best with the post. Never underestimate how important the image that goes with the post is. Facebook does give you the option to upload your own picture if you copy and paste the link direct to the page. The best size picture for this is 1200 x 627 pixels. Square pictures are better than rectangular ones.
- Consider doing a watermark on your pictures. A watermark of your site would just be the URL or name in text somewhere in the picture that does not distract from the image.
- Create a schedule to make sure you are not posting the same content too frequently.

If you have a new post, post it in the morning and then again in the evening. Some of your readers will have missed it previously. Don't bombard people but do share your good content with them, You don't need to just share new articles, share your best content every four-six weeks and also rotate seasonal posts and those that are very popular. You could also do reader questions. Share the less popular stuff too, make good use of your archive. We have over 5000 articles in our archive at Frost Magazine. It would be silly not to use them.

You can pay to promote your posts on Facebook if you feel it is worth it to you. Do keep in mind that unless you have an affiliate link in that post or are selling products it might not pay off financially for you.

Paying for Facebook advertising will probably pay off if you have a product to promote, want to attract new Facebook likes, have something to sell or to build your email list. Facebook advertising can be a powerful tool. Having a lot of Facebook likes also helps you negotiate with brands and advertisers.

How to run a Facebook Promotion.

Go to your Facebook business page. Click 'create ads' and then choose the option that you want to run your ad for. The options are: page post engagement, clicks to website, website conversions, app installs, app engagement, event responses or other claims.

Next, write the text and choose your picture. Facebook will use your page wallpaper automatically. You can also add more pictures. Start with an enticing picture. Next you choose your demographic, getting this right is key. You can custom the audience by age, gender, location, language, interests and behaviours. You can also target the ad to people who have friends who already like your blog. If you want you can make it that the ad only reaches people who match that criteria. Finally, you then choose your budget and timeframe for your ad. The more you narrow it down and target your audience the more powerful your ad will be. When it comes to selling something or signing up to your newsletter it could pay to advertise to the people who already like your page. You could also make a list of people who have already signed up to the newsletter. It is a waste of money if you are doing the promotion to get more email sign ups and you are reaching people who have already signed up. Create a custom audience and exclude these people. Facebook advertising can be affordable and you will also be able to customise to reach your target audience.

Pinterest Strategy

Pinterest is the third largest social media site with Facebook and Twitter ahead of it. While Pinterest may look merely visual it tends to covert to readers. Use it properly and you could get thousands of people come to your site. The thing about Pinterest is that it is all about sharing great content. Pinning and re-pinning. They want great ideas and articles and pictures that they can share and read. Research also indicates that people are more likely to buy something and view more pages than people on Facebook. Pinterest has more than 85 million users. It is not to be underestimated.

Get more Pinterest followers, more traffic.

Turn the people who click through into loyal readers.

Improve your Pinterest Home page. Make your Pinterest name your blog name unless your name is similar to that of your site. Take time to write your description. Make it interesting but also make sure it describes your blog accurately. Make sure you include the URL to your blog. Use a picture of yourself or your blog. Pinterest uses square profile pictures. Next, work on your boards, make sure that each one represents a category in your blog. The more niche these categories the better. Don't just do a food board, break it down into sections: desserts, mains etc. The more niche your boards, the more likely they will be found and followed and the pictures in them will be pinned. You can list your boards alphabetically or by category. Make sure that every board has a stunning cover that draws people in. You want everything to be beautiful and visually stunning. Make sure each board has a great description and that every board has been categorised.

Do a 'Best of' board full of all the of the best posts on your blog. Put it at the top of your page.

You need a constant stream of high-quality posts. Go through all of your old posts, add better pictures and edit the content. Delete anything that drags the site down. Change the title of any pictures to make them more engaging and searchable.

Use collaborative boards which are active and large. Accept invitations from any and add images to the ones that you are already a part of. This gives you access to a whole new set of readers and traffic growth. Pinning to these boards will also not show up in your feed so won't overwhelm your readers. Join as many collaborative boards as you can and pin away. Make sure they are active and have a high number of followers. To join some you can politely ask some friends to add you to groups they are part of. Watch out for open groups you can request to be invited to or email Pinterest users asking them to add you, saying how much you love their board. See if there are any Pinterest collaborative Facebook groups which you can join. You can also start your own and invite people to join. The more you invite other people the more they might return the favour. On the busiest board, try to pin your best content once a day and vary the times.

Pin other people's content to your boards, too. Don't pin the same stuff to a lot of different boards. You can do so afterwards, and probably should, but don't do it immediately. The people who follow all of your boards will see lots of duplicate content. You don't want all of your recent pins to be the same either. Pin your best content to lots of different collaborative boards regularly. This will get you new streams of traffic.

Do all you can to share your best content with as many people as possible. The more pins the better.

The right combination of great content, a brilliant image, a good description, then well-marketed to as big an audience as possible equals viral traffic. Viral traffic does not have to be about luck.

Social media can waste a lot of your time so use it wisely. Place the right keywords in your image description so people can find your image when they search for pictures on that subject on Pinterest. Always optimise your pictures.

Make your board look good. Pinterest is obviously a visual medium.

Pin pictures from other sites. Don't just self-promote.

Share your pins on your other social media accounts.

Update regularly but make sure the content is relevant and entertaining. Consistency is important. Update throughout the day, not all at once.

Like other people's pins and always interact with people.

Find good content and share it.

You can pin video too. Share video from your blog and YouTube channel. You can even make a specific introduction video about your blog.

You can allow other people to pin to your boards by making them contributors.

If you link to your Facebook account, Pinterest will add your Facebook friends to your Pinterest feed and include a link to your profile.

TURNING CASUAL READERS INTO LOYAL READERS

Twitter: follow brands and blogs you like. Participate in conversations. Retweet and favourite. Be generous.

Do Twitter and Facebook competitions to raise followers.

It is never a good idea to focus on getting one source of traffic. Try to be as diverse as possible to protect yourself.

I use a WordPress template and you can choose for your posts to be automatically shared on Facebook and Twitter. This is great and cuts down on work but sometimes the picture just doesn't work so always share the post again with a better picture. It is more likely to be read if you do. Always make sure that the app is automatically posting your updates. These apps that automatically share things stop working occasionally so always check every now and again to make sure they are still working. Days can go by and you will have lost traffic and it will look like you have not updated your blog.

Platforms to reach more people on:

- Quora: you ask or answer questions.

- Blog posts

- Udemy. Video courses.

- Email newsletter.

- Public speaking.

- Webinars

- Workshops

- Social media: LinkedIn, Facebook, Twitter, Pinterest, etc.

- Books.

- YouTube videos.

- Slideshare presentations.

- Podcasts.

QUORA

Use Quora to promote your blog. Answer questions that are related to your blog audience. Provide good, thought-out answers. Show that you know what you are talking about. Don't be too self-promotional; people don't like being sold to. People can upvote answers and blog posts on Quora so the better your answer the more likely it is to get upvoted and then the more exposure you get. To get more traffic to your blog, link to relevant articles contextually within your answer. Make sure you include a link to your blog on your Quora profile. When you answer a question the name and the brief biography of the person is included so include a link to your blog in your biography.

Another thing to keep in mind when using Quora is that when your answers and posts get upvoted you get Quora credits. You also get Quora credits when you answer questions that people ask you, when someone answers something you asked and it gets upvoted and when people follow questions that you ask. You can then use these credits to promote your answers and your blog posts. The best thing is that, although these credits mean your answer appears in the newsfeed of all of the people who follow that topic in a similar way to promoted tweets on Twitter, it is completely free, and you just need to get upvoted.

If you want you can cross-post your blog posts on Quora. This will attract a wider audience but you might get less traffic to your actual blog, so keep that in mind. Your blog posts on Quora will show up in search results on Quora and can also rank highly in Google. Quora has a large audience so it is definitely worth getting your name out there on it. Even if you just ask a question and answer some questions. The people on Quora are also engaged so you could make some great connections.

YouTube

YouTube is the second largest search engine. It is owned by the largest search engine, Google. It is also the third most visited site in the world. Because YouTube is owned by Google, the videos on there also tend to rank well in search results. Use this to your advantage. Always tag videos properly and share them.

Produce good content that your readers will love and that is valuable to them. Use keywords so they will find it and make sure to mention your blog in your videos and include a link on your channel and even in the description.

Join the Mumsnet Bloggers network. This is good SEO as your posts will be on mumsnet.com and could also be shared on their social media.

Slideshare: presentation hosting network on which you can upload PowerPoint, PDF, Keynote and Open Document presentations. If you use it then make sure you include a link to your blog in your profile, your presentations description and also in the actual presentation. The handy thing is that viewers can click on the links within a Slideshare presentation.

Always deliver value.

The goal of Facebook's EdgeRank algorithm is for people to see the highest quality content. I also read that memes and quotes are now getting penalised no matter how many likes they get. So that is something to keep in mind.

Building an Email List.

You can build an email list in the following ways: adding people to it that you have worked with, adding people that will be interested and giving new people the option to sign up. I would be very careful when it comes to adding people to your list. A lot of people won't like it and you could get a reputation as a spammer.

After you have an email subscriber base you can send a newsletter, an e-edition of your blog, news, special offers, event information or anything else you think will be of interest. Don't email people too much though. People are very busy and this will probably make them unsubscribe. Remember: always provide value.

FeedBurner will let you send an email to subscribers for every article you post. If you want people to receive the full article, not just a snippet, when FeedBurner sends them your post, go to Settings on your WordPress dashboard and go to Reading, then select 'Full text' where it says 'For each article in a feed show.'

MailChimp will let you send whatever you want, not just posts. You do it through MailChimp after installing the plugin on your blog to get people to sign up. Make your email subscribe button as visible as possible. Offer something free to people who subscribe. MailChimp and AWeber offer advanced auto responders but you might have to pay for a premium service. FeedBurner lets you do this for free. Go to your account on FeedBurner, click on publicise and then email subscription, then click on your communication preferences. From here you can edit your opt-in message and include any links. Of course, people might just take the free thing and not activate their subscription so it isn't perfect. Hopefully people won't be so unscrupulous.

Use AWeber or MailChimp so people can sign up and be notified each time you post something new.

HOW TO GET MORE PEOPLE TO SIGN UP TO YOUR NEWSLETTER.

Make sure the newsletter sign up is in a prominent place on your blog, display the email opt in at the end of each blog post, offer something free in exchange for a sign up.

The best way to build up your email subscriber list is to provide amazing content they will want to read.

Twitter.

In the past few years Twitter has entrenched itself into our everyday lives. It is how I found out Kate Middleton was to marry Prince William, and that Christopher Hitchens had died. Twitter is now how most people get their news. It is also a brilliant marketing tool. No matter what you do with your life, you can improve your career and be in contact with people from all around the world. Here is how to grow your Twitter audience.

Go for quality, not quantity.

Some people may have thousands of followers, but they may be spammers or may have paid for them. (Buying followers is against Twitter's terms and conditions.)

Try to not get upset when people unfollow you. It is usually not personal. Maybe you retweet too much, maybe they are just following too many people. It has nothing to do with you as a person. Just unfollow them back, unless they are incredibly interesting.

Add your photo and professional details to Twitter. People are more likely to follow you if they know a bit about you. Brevity is the soul of wit and even more important on Twitter. You only have 140 characters to get your point across. It is a good skill to have.

Hash tags
Which is this: # (to get a hash tag on a Mac Alt + 3 = #) This creates, in Twitter's words, a 'global conversation' that everyone can follow.

Put a follow button on your blog or website

Remember, you can only direct message people who follow you, and they can only do the same if you are following them.

Interact with people.

Follow people. They might follow you back. You can follow 2,000 people initially, more if you have over 2000 followers.

- Be worth following.

- Have a good avatar. A picture of yourself is good.

- Have a good bio. Keep it short and interesting.

- Post interesting stories. Add links to articles you enjoyed reading.

- Add yourself to directories like Wefollow.com

- Get your friends to follow you.

- Add your Twitter to the signature in your email.

- Don't worry if it seems to be taking a while. Your Twitter will grow.

- Be interesting. That is the most important thing. If you are interesting people will follow you.

- Have a niche; tweet about a specific thing. You can grow your business and become an expert in your field.

- Join Klout.

- Don't buy Twitter followers. This might look good but what you want is engaged followers.

- Don't constantly retweet.

- Don't tweet all the time. If you clog up someone else's feed then they will probably unfollow you.

- Don't be offensive. Have your opinion but respect other people's.

- Respond to people.

- Follow other people in your field.

- Tweet regularly. Three times a day is fine.

- Remember that things came across differently in print. Sarcasm and humour can be taken seriously.

- Watch out for spam. Change your password and don't click on links from people you don't know.

- Be relevant.

- Don't try to please everyone. You have to have an opinion or you will not be interesting.

Use HTTPS for improved security on Twitter.

Tweet Reach is a program that shows you how many people each Tweet reached. Tweet Reach also lets you know what subjects your readers are most interested in.

Tweet at the right time: Between 10am and 4pm is the most popular time for Twitter activity. If you want to reach people all around the world, use a plugin like Tweet Old Post which I use on Word-Press. You can set it to automatically tweet your old posts on a timer of your choosing. Once an hour etc.

Always interact with followers.

Follow and interact with influential Twitter users. We had Perez Hilton share one of our articles when we started and it got a lot of hits and was a stamp of approval for our site. Follow relevant people and interact with them. You never know, they might retweet or respond to you. This will create buzz around your account and give you an air of legitimacy. Grab their attention.

Follow targeted people. You want the followers of the people who blog in your niche. Follow their followers.

Use tools like Tweet adder, Flash tweet and Market me tools.

Unfollow unresponsive people. Twitter sets limitations between the ratio of followers and how many people you follow. If the number of people you follow exceeds the number who follow you your account could get locked and you won't be able to follow anyone else. You can use friendorfollow.-com for this. It lets you unfollow people who are not following you on Twitter and Instagram. It is completely free. You can also use ManageFlitter which allows you to unfollow people based on a number of factors including lack of activity, spam messages, non-English tweets and people who are not following you back.

Auto tweets are great. Make sure you have an app that will auto-tweet your posts.

Tweet Old Posts is great too, it tweets your old posts.

Don't be self-serving. Tweet and retweet other people's good content. Your feed should not just be about shameless self-promotion.

Share some personal information. Make sure you come across as a real person. You don't have to share information about your personal life or your kids, but share something about the books you have read, or some of your likes or dislikes. Just let people feel like they know you and your brand.

Twitter is always about connections. Thank people if they share your content, always reply to comments and questions (unless it is abusive or trolls) and offer to help other tweeters. Make sure you add personality to every tweet.

Always use hashtags when sharing on Twitter, some hashtags are more popular than others so do some searches to check whether or not you could get more readers by using a more active hash-tag. If you can use a hashtag that is trending, then even better. You can also @reply anyone who is mentioned in the post. Just make sure it is relevant and not spam. Click on certain hashtags and if you can connect with someone or help them with something then do so. Build connections. Don't be pushy or like a used cars salesperson. Connect to people, don't sell to them.

Give a free report or something for people who share your page on Twitter or Facebook.

To create a report, reuse a few blog posts about a specific topic, put them together in PDF form, give it a great title and go to fiverr.com and get an eCover.

BLOGLOVIN'

Bloglovin' is an excellent site where people can follow different blogs and see the posts from that blog in their Bloglovin' feed, along with the other blogs that they follow. Bloglovin' also send out an email with the top posts. You can get a button to put on your site to encourage people to follow you on it.

TIPS

- *Connect all of your social media accounts to each other. Put your social media accounts on your blog homepage.*
- *Use hashtags.*
- *Be interesting on social media. Engage with people. Join conversations. Get involved and always reply to people*
- *Social media is also a great place to get ideas for more article.*
- *Don't just post links.*
- *Engage well in conversation. Be honest and funny.*
- *Tweet photos and videos. Mix up the media, give your readers variety.*
- *Stay current.*
- *Do a competition. Get people to follow and retweet the competition to gain followers and exposure. Or like and share on Facebook.*

GOOGLE +

- Invite people into your circle.
- Follow people.

- Put them into relevant circles.

- Make your Google + profile look good. Upload a good picture and write a good description. Keep your audience in mind when writing your description. Tailor it to them.

- Post regularly.

- Share pictures and video.

- Promote your different social media accounts everywhere. Include them on your blogs sidebar.

- Comment on other people's Google +.

- Promote your Google + account like you would your other accounts.

- Refer to your social media accounts and ask people to follow you on them. Then follow them back.

Share each published post as a status update. Use relevant hashtags. Your posts will be seen by those in your circle. You can also post to communities. According to Moz (and they should know), the number of times a page is shared on Google+ is the second most influential factor on how it is ranked on search engines. So keep that in mind. Also, the links to your posts are also followed so posting to Google + also works as link building.

LINKEDIN

With LinkedIn you can also share on groups. This can be very handy indeed. You can even start your own group. I have found groups on LinkedIn to be quite active and engaged. Join lots of groups in your target niche. Share in them but also make sure you engage with people.

Also share your posts on LinkedIn, you can do this through your social sharing buttons on your blog (make sure you have some!). Your posts will be seen by people in your network but also by the network of anyone who has liked your update.

FORUM MARKETING

Provide quality comments and mini-posts, answer people's questions and try to solve their problems, support people, link to other threads. Develop a reputation as someone who is an expert in their field. Check which topics and threads are popular and then provide more of the same. Solve a very specific problem. Reply to every comment and it will even bump up your post.

Go the extra mile.

Offer shareable content.

YOUTUBE

Create videos full of useful tips. Keep them single concept and don't overwhelm people with too much information. People have short attention spans. Do videos 2-3 minutes long on a single topic. Have a uniform style. Ask people to subscribe at the end of the video. Ask them to like the video too. Tell them to feel free to put any comments below.

Check out how other people market on YouTube. Encourage viewers to check out the blog for more info.

PODCASTING

Doing podcasts is another way to reach people. You should have the software to make these on your computer. People feel like they know you when they listen to you.

In your podcasts you could interview other people in your blog/niche/industry

Link to other bloggers, create a 'best of' list on a certain topic, write about a good post another blogger wrote, do interviews on a specific topic or do a case study.

Check your traffic through Google Analytics. Go to traffic sources, sources- all traffic. Focus on traffic sources, average visitor duration and bounce rate. The bounce rate is the number of people who go to your site and then leave only reading one page. The lower the bounce rate, the better. Analyse what is working and what isn't. Focus more on what is working, drop what isn't.

CHAPTER 9: FURTHER TIPS FOR BUILDING YOUR BLOG

After you have made sure your design is great and that your blog is full of amazing content you can start building it up. Here are some ways.

WORD OF MOUTH

Tell your friends and family about your blog. They will probably be your first readers. Then share your blog on your Facebook, Twitter, Pinterest, Google + and every other social media site you are on. This is basic but can get things moving. This was also how I started my site, Frost Magazine, and some of those people are still reading it six years later. Do an elevator pitch for your blog. If you don't know what that means it is basically a 30-second pitch describing your blog, what it is about and why people should read it. You can even send an email to your contacts announcing the launch (or re-launch if you have been doing it for a while) of your blog. Or invite them to read your latest blog post and don't forget the link! You could also ask for feedback.

Have some good business cards printed and start handing them out. Vistaprint and moo.com both make good, inexpensive business cards.

- Share your posts on all of your social media.
- Ask friends and family to spread the word.
- Always think of your blog as a business.
- Always improve your product through market research.

Do a blog hop. A blog hop is a collection of links on one blog or a group of blogs which gets bloggers to connect and support each other. You link your blog and then visit the other blogs that are linked; they then do the same for you. It is also called a link party. As your blog grows this will probably be too much work as you will have a million other things to do, but this is a great way to get some traffic for your blog and get known outside of your own circle. It is also a great way to network with other bloggers and become part of a supportive community. A link party is the same thing but is individual posts, usually within a certain genre. It can be time consuming but try a few and see if it drives traffic to your blog and gets you new readers.

Link parties are a lot of work, they take up a lot of time and you have to promote them and invite people to join. Make sure it is worth the time, effort and commitment. Running a blog is hard work and there will always be something that needs done. If something is either not working, or not giving enough back for the amount of work involved, then move onto something else. You are only one person, do not exhaust yourself.

Comment on bigger blogs to drive traffic to your blog. It does work. Just don't be spammy or rude. Share insightful comments that add to the conversation. Don't try to spam the traffic that other, bigger blogs get, it is not nice and you don't want to get a bad reputation. Just do some insightful comments that add to the conversation and don't comment too much or become an annoyance.

The best thing to do is to go to blogs that you genuinely love and comment on posts that interest you. As long as you do this in a genuine way it won't come across as spam, nor matter that your URL is in the comment.

SUPPORT OTHER BLOGGERS

Another way to build goodwill, a community and (hopefully) some traffic is to link to other bloggers, feature and promote them. If that blogger has a 'trackback' feature enabled on their site they will also be notified that you have linked to their post.

You can also do a roundup feature based on one idea or news story. Collecting different views on the same thing from many blogs and linking to them. You can throw a link party based on a theme or you could do a photo collage on Pinterest and link to each picture. The opportunities are endless.

HOST GUEST POSTS AND GO TO BLOGGING EVENTS.

Some tips:

- Make connections.
- When you don't know what to say, ask a question.
- Don't overdo it.
- Engage.
- Hand out your business cards.

- But make conversation first. It really turns people off when you just bomb them with your card and then walk off.

- Listen more than you speak. This is the best way to connect with people, and also to learn.

- Work on your friendships.

- Always email the people who have handed you their business cards. Otherwise the time and effort is wasted and that person just becomes a lost contact. Email the person saying where you met them and how nice it was, include a titbit from your meeting and ask them to stay in contact. Follow them on Twitter or friend them on Facebook.

When it comes to writing guest posts on other blogs, make sure they are so good that readers will then flock to your site to read more of your work and hopefully become a fan.

Ask for guest post guidelines.

This is better than just blindly submitting a post. Successful blogs get hundreds of emails a day and capturing their attention is hard. Making the extra effort will be noticed and improve your success rate.

Be clear.

Your readers may know you and your background but when you do a guest post you are writing for a completely new audience. Don't make assumptions and write in a clear, concise way.

Don't make your guest post an advertisement. Selfish self-promotion is a huge turn off.

Submit good content.

For guest posts on your blog: don't be scared to ask for revisions to a post if you don't think something matches your site, the style, format and tone. Always think of your readers. Make sure anything they submit is original content. Duplicate content gets you penalised by Google.

BUILDING AN EMAIL LIST.

Actively build your subscriber list.

Do competitions and make a condition of entry subscribing to the newsletter. Put a widget on your sidebar making it easy to subscribe to your newsletter. Make sure you put it in a prominent place.

Offer something free to those who subscribe. This can be anything from a free e-book, a workbook, some information or a guide.

Promote the incentive on social media: write a post about the free thing you get when you sign up to the newsletter and share it across your social media a lot.

lead-pages.net allows you to create opt-in pages which you can then pay to share on Facebook.

Ask people to subscribe on a semi- regular basis. It usually takes more than once to get them to sign up but put the idea in their head and eventually they should sign up if they love your content.

hellobar.com allows you to make free customisable bars and then put them on your site.

I love MailChimp. It is free and easy to use. Others you can use are MadMimi, AWeber and Infusion-Soft.

WHEN OTHER PEOPLE DO GUEST POSTS FOR YOU

Anyone who does a guest post for you will get more traffic as these people will promote it. It will get you new readers and give your readers something new. Unless it is a company or business let them link to their blog or whatever they are promoting, like a book.

Testimonials. When posting testimonials, make it more about the client than you. What people are saying about how great you are? Ask for testimonials. Include a link to their site. Say something like 'Thank you for the great testimonial. We love our customers.'

Split longer posts into parts posted over a few days. You could also gain subscribers by asking people to subscribe to be alerted about the next post.

Ask people to subscribe. At the end of each post encourage readers to sign up.'If you would like to receive our monthly e-edition then sign up. We won't sell your details'. Ask people to subscribe and show them how. You can use Feedburner for this.

Put your blog on these directories: http://www.thelinkmedic.com/2010/09/over-25-great-sites-to-submit-your-blog.html

Ask your readers what they want. You can do this on one of your social media accounts or by doing a survey on Survey Monkey or another site.

Fulfil a need.

Write a guest post for another blog: make sure it is informative, inspiring, educational, funny and/or useful. Make sure the guest post is never purely self-promotional. Always offer something. Promote yourself in the author bio. Include a link to your site.

To get a guest post, send a brief, concise email to a blog that you read a lot or one that is within your niche. You could also ask your supporters/customers if they would like a guest blog. Make sure the post is already written and ready to go.

Write nice things about other people and brands. Build contacts.

TIPS ON WORKING FROM HOME

HAVE A DESIGNATED AREA.

It helps to have a designated area where you work. A desk is best but it could be the kitchen table or even on the couch with the TV on (no judgement here, I have done it!). Truth is, I change my designated area. I have a desk I work at a lot but we also have a huge kitchen table I work at. In winter when it is very cold and we only heat one room I work in our bedroom, usually in my pyjamas. Wherever you work, make sure you are comfortable and that you have everything to hand.

TAKE BREAKS.

If you worked a real job you would get breaks. Legally your employer would have to give you a certain amount. Remember this! Just because you are your own boss doesn't mean you get to treat yourself like a slave. Taking breaks and making sure you have lunch also makes you more productive and keeps you healthy.

EAT AND KEEP HYDRATED

Be kind to yourself always. Make sure you drink enough water, snack and have as much tea as you want.

OTHER TIPS

Do your bookkeeping every three months. I don't always follow this advice and always regret it. There is nothing worse than a huge pile of receipts and invoices at the end of the tax year. You will thank yourself come tax time.

Don't sell yourself short. Know your worth and don't settle for less.

HOW TO RUN A SUCCESSFUL BLOG WITHOUT BURNING YOURSELF OUT.

There is always so much to do when it comes to blogging that it is easy to be overwhelmed, or just think that there is no way you could possibly do it all. Here are my tips to making it work without giving up your life.

STAY ORGANISED

This is key and very important. You must keep organised. How you do this is up to you but there are many different ways. Keep track of both your short and long term goals.

Expenses, deadlines, schedules, recipes, to-do lists, editorial calendar, login info, post ideas, income from various sources, contacts, traffic statistics, social media, pictures, emails, dealings. There really is a lot to keep track of when you run a blog.

Try planners, calendars, spreadsheets, even Google docs to help you manage it all.

Think of your long term goals and focus on the bigger picture. Keep your long term goals short and limit the number. This way they will be less overwhelming and more motivating.

Have a year at a glance page. For important events, themes in a certain month, sponsored posts, blog conferences, work events and family stuff.

Think of your personality and organise your life the way that works for you. If you are not an organised person then you will have to work harder and find a system that keeps everything in order. Remember: chaos is not a filing system.

Keep a record of everyone you meet, along with their details and where you met them. Include any key information or memorable things that were said or that happened.

Have a Good Support Team

Build a good team. I am very lucky with Frost. I have a number of great team members. One of whom is best-selling author Margaret Graham who is our contributing editor. She is amazing, getting the word out and bringing in a lot of amazing content. A lot of our writers, like Owun Birkett and Junior Smart have been with us since the beginning. Keshini Misha and Corinne Tuddenham-Trent are wonderful fashion and event writers who have contributed terrific articles. My husband has also written many of our most popular articles and is always giving great advice and suggestions. Blogging is like a black hole: you can put all of your time and effort into and it will still require more from you. When you start out you can ask friends and family to help. You can even get some contributors, the problem being is that you won't be able to pay them but do not let anyone make you feel bad or bully you about this. Because you won't be getting paid either! I have had a number of people be rude to me or even send me invoices, even when Frost had just started. Be as nice and polite as you can, no matter how aggressive they are. Explain, very gently but firmly, that even you don't get paid for working on your blog and that they knew that from the beginning. The move on. Don't let it upset you. If you cannot afford to pay people, then you cannot afford it.

When you are lucky enough to make enough money to hire help it will make a difference. A virtual or real-life assistant can help in many ways, from doing emails, social media, ad sales, negotiating with brands, managing the day-to-day running, bookkeeping. Whether or not you want a virtual or real-life assistant will be a matter of preference. If you run your own blog you will probably work from home, so keep in mind that the person will be in your personal space.

If you cannot afford to hire a complete team then hire someone who will work in the area that you hate the most, need help with the most, or are particularly weak in. Make sure you have a clear job description for your assistant. Always ask for references and make sure that person has experience in the area and is a hard worker. Do an interview even if it is over Skype. Ask around for recommendations. Hire them for a short project with a specific end to start with. See how they do and then hire them longer term if they do a good job. Make sure you communicate with your assistant and do performance reviews. Make sure the assistant makes the most of the time you are paying them for. If you are not happy with something talk to them about it first and then if things don't improve, find a new assistant. An assistant should make your life easier, not cause any stress. Make sure they are a good fit not just for your business, but also for you and your personality. Training the person is always a good idea, make the investment of time and money into the right person and they really are worth it.

When it comes to blogging, outsource when you can. This will help grow your business and pre-serve your sanity.

NETWORKING

Always offer something first. Do not be a taker.

When you catch someone's eye you have three seconds to say something interesting to make conversation with them.

Be helpful and expect nothing in return but this doesn't mean that you should constantly help peo-ple who offer nothing in return. Don't let people take advantage of you.

SUMMARISE RESEARCH YOU HAVE DONE

Let people know why you are qualified to write about your niche. List achievements and qualifica-tions in a non-imposing way. Offer unique and expert analysis. Be authentic. Let your personality and character shine through.

SHARING BLOG POSTS ALSO ALLOWS YOU TO STAY IN PEOPLE'S MINDS

Promote your network and the people in it. Give them a link back to their blog and share it on all of your social media. Build up a supportive network of people all looking out for each other. A rare and beautiful thing in this world.

TIPS FOR A FREELANCE LIFE

MANAGING YOUR TIME

Because there is just not enough time in the world, and there never will be, you will have to be-come a dab hand at time management. Here is the golden rule: always do the most important things first.

Anything with a deadline gets done first, advertising is to be prioritised. The best way to do things is to get the hardest and most important tasks done first. This way, even if the rest of the day you are a bit slow, you will still have gotten a lot done and will feel good about yourself. I tend to try and do three important things that I don't want to do every day.

It is so easy to get distracted by the internet, by social media and emails. It is also very easy to get drawn into debates on Facebook or Twitter, or to have trolls being mean so you feel you have to stand up for yourself. My productivity went up hugely when I decided that I would no longer get into arguments with strangers on social media. Never feed the trolls. Just agree to disagree politely. I tend to only go on Twitter once a day during workdays. This has greatly improved how much work I get done. I tend to do the same thing with Facebook. Also, don't feel the need to check your extensive blog stats every single day. Try once a week or month if you can. I check the hits everyday but that is all. Pinpoint the things that waste your time and tackle them one by one.

Focus on the work more than emails too. They can wait. Great content always comes first.

HERE ARE SOME MORE TIPS:

- Create a daily routine.
- Give yourself a certain amount of time to get each task done. Discipline is key.
- Do similar posts in bulk.
- Make a daily to-do list.
- Take breaks. Make sure you stretch and walk around a bit, too.
- Get rid of the unessential.
- Do the hardest thing first. Time is precious.
- Use auto-responses. If you get a lot of requests about something, create a standard post that you can then tweak.
- Delete all nonessential emails and don't feel you have to respond to every single press release you get, no matter how pushy the PR person is. You won't have time. Don't feel guilty about it. They get paid to send the press releases to you, you don't get paid to spend all day replying to them.
- Use folders to organise your emails. I do this and it saves a ton of time and makes things so much easier.
- Turn off all of your social media alerts. Including the ones on your phone. This will stop you getting distracted.

Know if you are a night owl or a morning person, then do the hardest stuff when you are more motivated and save the mindless stuff for the time when you will feel less alert and motivated.

The problem with running a blog is that there is always so much to do that you can never be done. There is no end of the day like there is in a 9-to-5 job. With blogging you can work anywhere, at any time and even while looking after your children. It gives amazing flexibility but you are always at work. This is why you must learn to switch off and know that your real life is just as important as your blog. My husband has been known to tell me off because I am still working at midnight, but I have gotten better and I also very rarely work on weekends now. This is also important because what will draw your readers in is being a real and genuine person. Not a robot who works all of the time. Life is a beautiful thing: live it. Be kind to yourself always and never worry about taking a break. This will stop you getting jaded. Give yourself permission to not get everything done.

Taking a break also gives you the time and space to see the bigger picture, and to stop before you burn out.

Running a blog is all-consuming and easy to get obsessed by but make time for friends, family and fun. This will help you, your health, your relationships AND your blog.

It is an amazing feeling when something you built from nothing starts to take off and becomes a proper business. When your blog becomes a business you become an entrepreneur. That's exciting, and it is a huge achievement. You may even become a name or a celebrity. You are now a brand. The world is your oyster. Think about all of the other things you could do.

CREATE A BUSINESS PLAN

Include all of the information about your business, what it does, your purpose, mission, goals and objectives. Have a concrete plan.

Business mission statement. Include a concise paragraph about what your business stands for and what it is about. Do this in two-three sentences.

Target audience: it is very important to understand your target audience and your market. Go into detail in this section. Include age, gender, interests, income, education, family status, etc. of your readers. Have as much information as you can. If you have more than one audience, include that. Also include a country breakdown. Frost Magazine has mostly UK and US readers but we are also read in pretty much every other country too.

Company assets: this will be all of your business assets. Everything it has going for it to generate revenue. The first thing will be your blog of course but you could also include social media reach, email list, classes…anything at all. List everything your business has going for it, even if it seems vague.

Core values: the personal beliefs of your business. These views will represent everything, from your employees to your actions. Keep them memorable and clear.

Long term goals. Include sales and growth targets. Uniques, email subscribers and social media followers. Always keep your long term goals in mind and include them in your business plan. Look forward five years. You can also do a two-year plan. Have the bigger picture in mind. Think about what you want to accomplish. Think about how your business will make a profit. Also think about your exit strategy.

Your short term goals should be the goals to reach the goals in your long term goals. Got that? Also include specific goals like higher revenue, sales and subscribers. Or more social media followers.

ACTION PLAN

Next you need to make an action plan. This can be in list form or broken down by months. Try to make these goals specific and clear. This will make it easier to implement them.

HOW TO GET MORE TRAFFIC

This is key, the more traffic you get the more successful you are, the more influential and the more money you earn. So how do you get more traffic? Here are some tips.

There is a principle created by Vilfredo Pareto that 80% of your results should come from 20% of your efforts. In other words: work smarter, not harder.

- Network like a pro.
- Be proactive.
- Write great content

- Market your site.

- Keep track of what is working and what isn't. Do more of what is. Use Google Analytics to analyse.

- Do a monthly review.

Comment on other blogs. Only respond to interesting posts and try to do some every day. Don't just do a 'great post' comment. Contribute something to the debate or discussion. You could also: ask a question (but don't be annoying!), answer a question (many bloggers end their post with a question), respond to another commentator, give an opinion, share something relating to the post. Stick to a small number of blogs in your niche when it comes to commenting. Doing up to 30 minutes a day is fine. You don't want to overdo it. Make sure the blog has a larger audience than you. Although if the blogger has hundreds of people commenting then you might get lost, use your best judgement to decide whether or not it is worth it. Commenting on up to twenty blogs is a good idea. You could also share the article that you comment on. This is a nice thing to do and is good karma. After you have built a relationship with them, or caught their attention you can email them and get in contact. The best way to do this is to join their mailing list. You can then reply to the newsletter they send you. Most bloggers get hundreds of emails every day and are more likely to respond to a subscriber than to an unsolicited email. When emailing start with a (genuine) compliment. Tell them about a post that you loved. If you didn't love their content and site then don't email them. Only make genuine contacts, don't be fake. Ask a question, give something back. Reciprocate. Don't be pushy. Meet for lunch or have a chat over Skype.

- Get blog traffic that converts into loyal readers and followers.

- Decide what you want people to do on your blog and prioritise it.

- Make it easy for people to share your content.

- Use an URL shortener. It makes it easier to share content on social media.

- Have a 'click to tweet' button on your site. It makes it easier to share content. https://click-totweet.com/

Offer readers something free to sign up to your newsletter or share your content. Offer a free report and they probably will. You can use Cloud Flood plugin for WordPress. It creates a catalogue of free reports.

Gravatar allows you to use the same picture when you comment on numerous blogs. This gives you brand consistency across the web.

Become friends with the top bloggers in your niche. Get their attention but don't be a stalker.

Write awesome posts for other blogs. It is obvious, but don't do this until you have some killer posts on your site. There is no point in writing guest posts to promote your site and writing skills and then people go to your blog and there is nothing there.

Be the best resource for a specific topic.

Creating a killer post. Lets do another quick breakdown on what makes a killer post. Make it scannable and easy to read. A reader should be able to know what your post is about just by scanning it. Don't use a big word when a small one will do and keep paragraphs and sentences short.

- Add multimedia. Use images, audio and videos to improve posts.
- Fact check and give specific examples.
- Link to other sites great content. Be generous.
- Write quotable lines and make them easy to share.
- Encourage engagement. Ask readers for their viewpoint.

Don't rely on search engine traffic because when Google do one of their algorithm updates you could find that your blog suffers.

Target a specific keyword. Use Google's keyword planner. Focus on keywords that get more than 1000 searches. Use phrases rather than just single words. You want long-tail searches. Include your main keyword throughout the article. In the title, URL, opening and end paragraph, main image, any sub-headings and the body of the article. Don't do this at the expense of the article. Write it well and make it readable. Include keywords but make them natural. If you use the Google keyword planner you will see that there are a number of phrases that are related to your keyword. Google places importance on something called Latent Semantic Indexing (LSI). This is an algorithm that takes different phrases and associates them with each other. It will make your post more findable if you weave 4 or 5 LSI keywords through your article. Diversify your search terms but not at the expense of good content. It's a skill, but you will learn.

Link to relevant articles. Link to other articles that are relevant to what you are writing. This will increase your authority to search engines.

Ping the search engines. Use Ping-O-Matic. Submit your RSS feed and then Ping-O-Matic will let the search engines know you have some new content on your blog.

Send an email to subscribers.

Ask the bloggers who you are friends with to share it. Always return the favour.

Use IM Automator to bookmark to multiple bookmarking sites. It costs $2.99 a month.

Post your content in relevant forums. Find forums through a search engine. Don't just go and spam a forum. Join and engage with people, link to other articles from good sites and reply to people.

Guest post. Use the audience and authority of the larger site to get more traffic to your site. Know where to post. Find the top blogs in your niche. Also find blogs that are in slightly different niches but are also relevant to your blog. Target people who you already have a relationship with first. Look at blogs and they should have information on guest posting. Follow it to the letter and you are more likely to be successful. Don't just target blogs with large audiences; also target ones with loyal readerships. Write for blogs that have a lot of people commenting as this is a sign that they have a lot of loyal readers. Less than 10,000 subscribers then it might not be worth it to you. Judge for yourself. You might just want to do guest posts for any blog you can. Go for blogs with an easy approval process too. It never hurts to make your life easier. Reach for the top. If you really love a blog and they are huge don't be scared to approach. Go for it!

Have an angle.

Read the content on the blog and target your post to them and their audience. Find a topic that the readers love and that will be popular. Do your research and look at their popular posts. Look at the posts that get a lot of comments, which posts have a lot of shares on social media and, if there is a 'most popular' widget, read the posts on it. The best thing to do is to try and match the topic of the post to that blog and your blog too. Hopefully readers will click through and become a reader of your blog too. Make sure your post has a great title. Have a hook. Solve a problem. Fulfil the promise you talked about in the hook.

Conclude the article with questions and a statement that builds engagement.

Make sure you get a by-line.

Get credibility and attention within your niche.

Exit Monitor is a conversion optimisation tool. Its software knows when a visitor is about to leave a page and then displays a pop up screen. This not only gives another page view but also allows you to offer the reader something for free or ask them to sign up to your newsletter.

Be polite. Be clear about what you want.

- Have an app.
- Go to iPad.
- Write books or do classes

Think about what social media your audience spends time on. Younger people are on Instagram. Find out where your customers hang out and go where they go.

You can email your blog post to people who you think will find it interesting. Just don't be annoying.

One of the brilliant things about blogging is how much you learn about so many different things: business, networking, design, writing, programming....the list is endless. Endlessly beautiful. You also meet amazing people.

Create a good impression. Make your blog looks good, have a tagline that describes your site and a good title. Have a well-organised navigational bar.

Take part in discussions on Reddit and submit links too. Respond to comments and upvote good comments about your article.

Attend industry events and network. Join diarydirectory.com for industry news, product launches and product requests.

Follow other bloggers and start a relationship with them. Comment on blogs and follow them on social media.

Use your logo constantly as an avatar all over your social media.

If you live in London you will get more event invitations and products sent to you as they can be sent via courier.

Lanyrd is an event directory service which connects social media networks and lets you know which of your contacts are going to certain events in different countries.

The Google Reader feed subscriber count is good for finding blogs to comment on.

Follow industry influencers on Twitter.

To find out who is linking to you just type link:domainname into Google. You can also use a plugin or various web services.

Social media is a tool to spread great content so have good content and the rest will come.

Write a list of the features you love on other bloggers' sites and put those features on your site.

Make Twitter lists. Give your list a name and put the bloggers you are following on that list. Give it a name like 'Top Tweeters' and they might even notice and be flattered.

Become an influencer.

As you get bigger you may need your own server and platform.

Google Keyword planner. Shows you how many searches each term gets a month and suggestions for other related keywords and phrases.

A great tool is Google's display planner. Work out the communities that your readers hang out in and sign up.

Don't join in until you can contribute usefully. Be a good web citizen. Don't spam, link drop or troll people.

CHAPTER 10: INTERVIEWS

I really hope you have enjoyed my book and it helps you become a successful blogger. Remember: you can achieve anything you want as long as you put one foot bravely in front of the other. Feel free to contact me or leave me any feedback via Twitter @Balavage or @Frostmag or email me via catherine@frostmagazine.com Also, wait for it … check out my blog! http://frostmagazine.com Good luck and stay in touch.

Name: Jessica Debrah

Blog: www.lookwhatigot.co.uk

How long have I been blogging for: 4 years yesterday! I started my blog on the 13th February 2011.

Describe your blog: Look What I Got is a fashion focused blog. I'm highly focused on showcasing my personal style, but I love to diversify and showcase my love of make-up and lifestyle quirky events.

Highest Point : Hmm that is tough, I can't pick one tbh. I would say being asked to speak at a variety of events, meeting Paul Solomons the Creative Director of British GQ, starting FBL Bloggers.

Lowest Point: Hmmm, I haven't really had any particular low points. When I'm stressed, I just take a break!

Favourite blog: Febgirl, In my Sunday Best, Discoveries if Self, Epiphannie A, Scarphelia, A Dash of Fash.

Inspiration: Is it a cop-out to say everything? I'm very visual and creative and I get inspired by lots of different things in London. I see the beauty in things and I am always getting ideas.

Top tips for bloggers: Have fun and post what YOU want. Your content makes you original and your blog is a space to showcase that. Never compromise that!

Do you make a living blogging?: Blogging is not my full time job. I make a living working in the digital and fashion industry. Hopefully when everything is in place I can make a living as a blogger.

FBL bloggers is my blogger network, with the aim of connecting all types of bloggers together. I started it 3 years ago and it has gone from strength to strength. We offer a haven for bloggers to network via the Facebook page and our Twitter @fashbeautylife. Additionally, we are starting to offer review and event opportunities. We grew exponentially due to our popular Twitter chat the #fblchat. The #fblchat runs from 8-9pm gmt every Tuesday. It is a great time to discuss important topics in blogging and to network with other bloggers.

I started it as I was frustrated with not knowing other bloggers. I was frustrated with the focus of only fashion and beauty bloggers and I wanted to give other bloggers who had strong content a voice!

You can get involved by joining our Facebook group, and following us on Twitter.

I'm working on a lot of projects, books, events and taking FBL bloggers to the next stage!!

https://twitter.com/fashbeautylife

https://www.facebook.com/groups/FASHBEAUTYLIFE

I interviewed a number of amazing female bloggers for an article I wrote for The Huffington Post. Read and learn from these amazing women.

Name Debbie Djordjevic

Blog www.thelife-edit.blogspot.com

How long have you been blogging for? About a year.

Describe your blog It's a general lifestyle blog written by a woman in her late forties. We are under-represented in the blogosphere but just because you hit a new marketing demographic doesn't mean you somehow 'die'. I am as interested in fashion, beauty, food and popular culture as I was twenty years ago, I just have an older (but not necessarily wiser) take on things. I write for women like me and to show the younger generation that ageing is nothing to be scared of and can actually be enjoyed. I have late teenage daughters who keep me young but I don't want to be them, we just learn from one another really. I like finding products that I think work and are relevant and I will pass those on. I hope I inform and inspire and also entertain, but I write it for me as an aide memoir as much as anything - I have been known to visit my own blog for a recipe I've loved rather than search for it again through my numerous cookbooks.

How did you get started? Well, working at Handpicked Media with so many blogs I felt I needed to really understand a blogger's perspective and the only way to do that was to start one myself. I am a journalist by trade and this is a very different kettle of fish.

Highest point? Seeing my traffic grow considerably once I came out of the Google search sandbox and everyone could find me. Having people respond to posts - though I must admit this tends to happen on my Facebook page or on Twitter rather than on my blog.

Lowest Point? Clearing off all the spam comments which are written to try to fool me - I've been around too long to be fooled!

Favourite blog? Now I am not going to get into trouble with all my brilliant blogger mates out there, but I can tell you the first blog I read was www.lileks.com which is an American journalist's blog which makes me laugh out loud and gives me insight into American life. I started reading him as far back as 2002 so I have been aware of blogging for a long time.

Inspiration? The many, many blogs I come across in my day job. I admire their passion, tenacity and the fact that they have gained audiences by tapping in to what people want to read.

Top tips for other bloggers? Keep going and don't do it for the money. It's a brilliant way of getting exposure, proving that you have opinions worth sharing, making friends, and gaining experience, just don't expect to necessarily be able to give up the day job. Some can, but the vast majority should do it for fun and to share a voice.

Do you make a living blogging? No and I wouldn't want to. I have spent 20 years making a living from either writing or editing and this is a blessed release. The freedom to blog about a wide range of topics and to give my own opinion is worth more. If I was younger I may think differently and I'm in awe of those who manage to make a living, don't get me wrong - and lots of them keep their credibility and unique voice while doing so - it's just not the reason I blog.

Name: Carrie Barclay (aka Queenie)

Blogs

DIGITAL bungalow -- www.digitalbungalow.co.uk

Kitchen Bitching -- www.kitchenbitching.co.uk

How long have you been blogging for?

DIGITAL bungalow launched in June 2011 and Kitchen Bitching launched in November 2011.

Describe your blogs

DIGITAL bungalow is a conglomerate of creative minds. Technically a lifestyle blog, Db features everything from art to restaurant reviews; wedding inspiration to fashion photography ... and many other subjects in between. We want DIGITAL bungalow to be a source of inspiration so if it inspires you in some way, we'll feature it!

Kitchen Bitching is a cookery site like no other; aimed at enthusiastic amateur cooks with some knowledge but in need of a friendly, helping hand from fellow enthusiasts.

All amateur cooks know the pain of a recipe that just won't do as it's told. Like a disobedient puppy it sulks, sticks, slides or sinks at that crucial moment just as your mother-in-law is rap-rapping on the door.

Kitchen Bitching is here to provide an open forum for amateur cooks to bitch about their culinary woes, rave about their kitchen triumphs and get hints and tips from the very best source - other cooks!

How did you get started?

I write for a living, and my partner is a photographer. DIGITAL bungalow was simply an opportunity to write about anything and everything that inspired myself and my partner. Very quickly we caught the bug and we were, for a time, posting at least once a day. When Kitchen Bitching was born we reduced our posts on Db to allow us to focus on KB, and now DIGITAL bungalow and Kitchen Bitching run harmoniously alongside each other.

The idea for Kitchen Bitching came about during a bitching session in our kitchen about a cake recipe that wasn't playing ball! Within days the site was designed and live, and we haven't looked back! We appointed an Editor about a month after launch and we've now got 12 regular contributors and an ever-growing number of loyal, enthusiastic readers.

Highest point?

The highest point to date has to be when DIGITAL bungalow was incorporated as a Limited Company. What started as a little pastime has now become a bona fide business and we're thrilled to be in talks with people about running events for bloggers, and I've recently been headhunted as a consultant for KAPOW Consulting to help new bloggers and small businesses enter into the blogosphere.

Lowest point?

When we were trying to keep up the momentum of posting every single day and I felt that Db was losing its focus. It was a difficult time. I all but gave up on the project, until my wonderful partner (in business and in life) sat me down and told me where I was going wrong. In blogging there's sometimes no one to rein you in or monitor what you're doing, so it's fantastic to work alongside someone who you trust to get the best out of you and not let you wander too far off-track.

Favourite blog?

Other than my own (of course!) my absolute favourite blog in the world is A Beautiful Mess (http://abeautifulmess.typepad.com/). The design, the subject matter, the photography and the aspirational nature of this blog means I can lose myself for hours in its folds and crevices. Elsie Larson really knows her stuff and her approach is friendly warm and inviting - A Beautiful Mess is a lovely place to spend time.

Inspiration?

Db is inspired by everything we come into contact with that gets us excited! On a personal level as a blogger I do really admire Elsie Larson of A Beautiful Mess and Sian Meades of Domestic Sluttery (for whom I was a columnist until recently); both ladies are such established, professional bloggers flying the flag for female bloggers and businesswomen everywhere.

Kitchen Bitching is inspired by every man, woman and child out there who wants to be able to cook up a storm in the kitchen but invariably ends up sitting under a table with a tea towel over their heads having a little weep (or is that just me?!). Again, on a personal level I have to say that Holly Bell (of Great British Bake Off fame) is a truly inspirational woman. We've been lucky enough to work with Holly on a number of features on Kitchen Bitching - she's such a down-to-earth, realistic person and, my word, can she cook!

Top tips for other bloggers?

Be nice! Bloggers have a bit of a reputation in certain industries for having a rather inflated sense of self-importance. The world doesn't owe you a living, and PRs aren't there just to give you free stuff. If you got into blogging for the freebies then may I politely suggest you get out now! Blogging is about personal opinion, self-expression and having a creative outlet. Sure, sometimes people will want to offer you nice things, often for free, but remember that these are a privilege, not a right.

Find clarity. Your blog is like your baby. You won't be able to see its sticking-out ears or unfortunately shaped nose. To you your blog is perfect, but make sure you have some people around that you trust to let you know if you're moving down the wrong path or wandering off on a tangent. A blog is an ever-evolving entity, but if you're simply revolving with no real purpose then you'll struggle to engage your audience.

Remember the photos! Images are SO important in a blog - we all spend so much of our time on computers for work and pleasure that a break from big chunks of text in the form of clear, well-composed, engaging pictures is a sure-fire way of getting readers coming back for more!

Do you make a living blogging? How do you make a living from blogging?

DIGITAL bungalow is now a Limited Company so we now do make money from what we do - although not purely from the sites on their own - we make money through using our reputation as bloggers to help new bloggers and small businesses set up social media platforms, through organising events and we also offer sponsorship deals and partnerships to a very select number of companies that we admire and respect.

Name: Shimelle Laine

Blog: pretty paper. true stories. www.shimelle.com:

How long have you been blogging for?

I started blogging informally via livejournal in 2002, and transitioned to a more professional blog in 2006. That blog soon started to present itself as something that needed more time than I could devote as just a side project, so in 2007 I took a year out from my job (as Head of English in a secondary school) to try the blog business full time, and I've yet to go back.

Describe your blog

I write a very niche blog in the crafting world, with a focus on scrapbooking. My blog itself includes a range of articles to cover new craft products, how-to videos and discussions on the merits of documenting everyday life through photos and writing. I also offer premium content in the form of online workshops through paid subscription.

How did you get started?

I got into scrapbooking as a hobby while at university, and not long later picked up some freelance work for specialist magazines, which was always just a bit of work now and then, but it grew year on year and gave me the opportunity to lead workshops at weekend retreats for crafty women. I found that keeping a personal blog, mostly read by close friends, made me want to update my website often but it was such a hassle in the format of a traditional site, so I added a blog format to make it easier to share finished projects, really. As soon as I added that element, I got requests to teach my workshops in more places than were viable and I felt horrible that I kept having to say I couldn't make it to every town requested, which made teaching online a logical next step.

Highest point?

Going full time in 2007, then being able to be the household earner from 2010, allowing us take on some seriously big travel. Then letting my husband work on a project that wouldn't have a regular income.

Lowest Point?

Although my posts are less about the details of my own life than many female bloggers, it is very personal in that I blog things I have made for myself. Because of that, it is often hard to separate criticism and I have had a few times when I took something so personally that I felt I couldn't continue. I'm thankful I've not lost my love of craft along the way, as it is very common for people in creative industries to stop enjoying it when they transition from fun to work.

Favourite blog?

I really don't have a single favourite, and maybe that is odd. I love to discover a new blog then read it all up, like when you can't go to sleep because you've just started a really fabulous novel. But because I like to read that way, I often get a little overkill and I don't go back for a few weeks. I like to save up the posts and have a bit more depth to read at once so it feels like an extended conversation with the blogger. I also find these days I read more via links passed around on social media than just from my personal favourites, and I love how that has introduced me to new content in fields I probably wouldn't have found on my own. One day I followed a single link from a friend of a friend and ended up reading case studies in an entirely different field that inspired a pitch that became a big part of the work I do now - and it was all because I read a really rambling blog post by a friend of a friend of a friend.

Inspiration?

I work with a mix of regular features that repeat on certain days, topics assigned by companies I work with and things that I just get the urge to try or share in some way. That balance works really well for me - it gives me half routine, half flexibility. If I rely entirely on being spontaneous, I never get anything done and if I rely entirely on routine, it feels too monotonous to be worthwhile. I like that I approach things in a slightly different way to a lot of bloggers in my niche. Many are very much about the visual because it's craft, but I love the written word. I love the discussion that comes with a community of readers. So I am often inspired by how on one hand, this topic is quite literally just glue and pretty paper but on the other, there is quite a lot of philosophical goodness to be found, if one wants to consider it.

Top tips for other bloggers

Let the passion come first and the profit come later. Whenever I work with or meet groups of beginner bloggers, there are always so many who have decided they know they want to make a living blogging but they don't know what they want to blog about yet. That sounds like such a recipe for burn out to me. If you're only picking a certain topic to make money, how much can you really say about that topic? And at this point in the game, there is a blog on every topic out there, and the most profitable topics have a flooded market anyway. What makes this my perfect job is how I get to think and write and share about something I love doing even when I'm not paid for it, and it's something I would frankly love to write about even if I was pondering whether to pay for craft supplies or food. Whatever your passion is, then that is the topic for you. I think that's why fashion bloggers have such intriguing blogs: they loved putting together outfits and showing them to the world way before they started blogging about it. By blogging they just have a new, highly filtered and specific audience. So my biggest tip is always go into blogging for the passion. And also: punctuation is your friend.

Do you make a living blogging?

Yes! It's my full time job and I'm currently the sole earner in our household.

How do you make a living blogging?

Unlike most blogs in my niche, I don't sell traditional sidebar or banner advertising. I'm not entirely advert free in that I do earn from affiliate links when I recommend my favourite products. My main earning comes from teaching online workshops (with a subscription fee) and I also earn by contributing content to a few related sites (stores and manufacturers of craft products), which I also post on my blog.

Name : Simone Antoniazzi

Blog : The Bottom of the Ironing Basket http://thebottomoftheironingbasket.blogspot.co.uk

How long have you been blogging for? 3 years

Describe your blog : My blog is a mixture of things that inspire me, lifestyle and style images, my own thoughts on life, travel, style, London and family. It's a collection of anything & everything that I love and find interesting.

How did you get started? I was inspired by an American friend who had started her own blog.

Highest point? Probably right now, my readership is at its highest. Through my blog I have been invited to London Fashion Week, to go to Morocco and I am just starting work with a personal trainer! Discovering ability that I didn't know I had and finding out more about myself.

Lowest Point? I don't have one.

Favourite blog? A Cup of Jo http://joannagoddard.blogspot.co.uk/

Inspiration? Magazines, other blogs, travel, life in general.

Top tips for other bloggers: Blog about what you really genuinely love and find interesting, that way you will develop a style and your "voice" will really come through. Don't feel you have to be confined to one topic, I blog about whatever appeals to me and is going on with me right now. Being yourself and honesty is the key to longevity.

Do you make a living blogging? I earn money from it, not enough to give up the day job yet though!

How do you make a living blogging? I carry advertising and advertorials on my blog.

Name: Camilla Tillson

Blog: asensibleheart.blogspot.com

How long have you been blogging for? For about 2 years now

Describe your blog? It's definitely fashion based with lashings of baking and DIY projects and my own photography.

How did you get started? I saw a really lovely blog online which inspired me to start my own, it's so great because that's exactly what they are there for!

Highest point? The first time I was featured on a bloggers social networking site as one of their top fashion blogs, it's great when your blog gets noticed! and going to Bristol Fashion week for free with my blog! It's really nice to do something active for your blog and meet other bloggers similar to you.

Lowest Point? I'm not sure if I have had one yet, my blog is all on my own terms, so if I don't fancy blogging I won't force it.

Favourite blog? I have to say one of the first blogs I ever read unabellavitablog.com and 'a beautiful mess' everything on there is so inspiring!

Inspiration? A lot of things, the people around me, the city I live in and I'm inspired every day by my blog feed!

Top tips for other bloggers? Your blog is your own space, do your own thing and let it develop in its own time. Don't ruin the space with ads before you have enough traffic, enjoy it while you can. It's not all about stats and followers, mine started off as an online live journal and if people are interested in reading what I post, that's great!

Do you make a living blogging? Not currently, I wouldn't ever say no to sponsored posts if I felt it could benefit my blog and my readers. I know it's a touchy subject for people, but why not earn a little off doing something you enjoy, as long as you're doing it for the right reasons.

How do you make a living blogging? I'd probably say via advertising and sponsored posts, and I guess you can save money if you're sent clothes and other bits. I'm not too hot on this topic!

Name: Becca Day-Preston

Blog www.bdpworld.blogspot.com BDP World

How long have you been blogging for? Only since October: I'm a baby!

Describe your blog It's a place for me to put all my thoughts about makeup and fashion and nails, without boring my friends. I was shaky at first, not discussing 'important' stuff, and just putting up pics of my nails, but recently I've written about confidence, airbrushing, period shame (that's a thing, apparently) and abstinence education in the UK, as well as keeping up the nails and lipstick posts.

How did you get started? With bad quality pictures and a lack of serious know-how…!

Highest point? Sali Hughes from The Guardian endorsing my angry rant about National No

Makeup Day

Lowest Point? Getting an email from a follower asking why I don't "just lose a bit of weight" UGH!

Favourite blog? Feministing

Inspiration? Veronica Sawyer

Top tips for other bloggers. Do what you love! Don't chase followers or try to score freebies: just have fun with it.

Do you make a living blogging? No, and I think I never will!

Name: Emma Iannarilli

Blog: fashion-mommy.com

How long have you been blogging for? Since August 2010

Describe your blog: A fashion/shopping/beauty/lifestyle blog from a full time mom

How did you get started? I was Deputy head at a Primary school when severe post-natal depression forced me to quit my job. After six months in counselling I felt better, but was bored just being a wife and mother. I read an article in a magazine about blogging and decided this could give me a creative outlet. Hence Fashion-Mommy was born!

Highest point?

So many. Meeting heroes like Markus Lupfer and Stella McCartney. Being named as one of 2012's hottest blogs by Spreading Jam. Being named as Blogger of the month for Next, blogger of the week for M&Co and publisher of the month for Boden. Being invited to an Evans photoshoot for their Autumn/Winter 2011 catalogue - just so many!

Lowest Point?

I tend to blog at night so I get very little sleep. Juggling the blog as a full-time job, with a demanding child not yet in school can be exhausting,

Favourite blog?

Big Fashionista is hilarious, and I love all of the Brummie Bloggers.

Inspiration?

Liberty London Girl, she was the first blogger I really noticed.

Top tips for other bloggers

Work at building your audience, use Twitter and Facebook to aid this, reply to comments to engage debate and discussion. Be original - let your personality shine through your work.

Do you make a living blogging?

I've just started to - it's taken a year and half to get to this point.

How do you make a living blogging?

Adverts, sponsored posts, text links, Skimlinks and affiliate links - but it's not a fortune!

Name: Anne-Marie - Ree for short

Blog http://www.reallyree.com/a

How long have you been blogging for? It will be 2 years in June.

Describe your blog - A personal lifestyle blog about the things I love across fashion and beauty. Face of the day, Outfit of the Day and lots of Product Review fun!

How did you get started? I started it as a hobby - and wrote a lengthy post about the differences of opinion between men and women on the subject of shoes!

Highest point? Working with BaByliss to make How To hair tutorials.

Lowest Point? There are always low days when it is hard to stay motivated but they never last.

Favourite blog? I love BritishBeautyBlogger.com to make sure I am up to date with all things beauty, and have a giggle!

Inspiration? Everything I see and try inspires me. I have started to actually think in blog posts!

Top tips for other bloggers - Stay connected, build your network and always talk to people.

Do you make a living blogging? Yes

How do you make a living blogging? By working with brands on a project basis.

Name: Aisling

Blog: fash-ling http://www.fash-ling.com

How long have you been blogging for? A year

Describe your blog: It's mainly my style, what I wear and what influences my fashion choices but I also include some beauty bits

How did you get started? I read a lot of the international blogs for years and when a friend started hers I was introduced to the UK blogging scene

Highest point? Pretty much any time someone new decides to follow me!

Lowest Point? Well trying to deal with HTML, I am useless and I find it so frustrating!

Favourite blog? Frassy

Inspiration? The catwalks, magazines, girls on the street and other blogs of course!

Top tips for other bloggers: Just keep doing what you love, that's all that matters

Do you make a living blogging? No, I do occasionally get sent items or invited to events which is truly an honour

Name: Lenka Silhanova

Blog: Acting Abroad - http://lenkasilhanova.blogspot.com

How long have you been blogging for?

Over a year.

Describe your blog? I'm sharing my experience of becoming an actress abroad, sharing tips and creating a community of people with the same goal. I think it's important for us actors to stick together and help each other out, as I've learned a lot myself by reading other people's blogs. This is a way for me to give back as well as to meet like-minded people and keep myself motivated and goal-oriented.

How did you get started?

I've been playing with the idea of starting a public blog for quite a while, since I've been keeping a private journal for several years, yet I was intimidated by the whole concept of opening my life and career out there in the world.

The first few months were the worst as I was still figuring the whole blogging thing out and writing in English, my second language, wasn't easy too. But I love the language so much it pushes me to constantly work on improving it. I found that I've learned so much by just by sitting down and writing, but also by reading A LOT of blogs, websites (that are edited) and, of course, books.

After a few months I've really gotten into blogging and I find it now, after a year of blogging, very fulfilling. I also find it to be a great marketing tool, till I'm ready to have my own website, this is a way to showcase my work both as an actor and blogger.

Last but not least reason to blog is that it's a form of storytelling, which is what I've chosen to dedicate my life to and this is a way of having it in my life without other people's permission. It's taking a part of my career I have the control of in my own hands and being proactive.

Favourite blog?

That's a tough question, there are so many great blogs I don't even know where to start. I love the Actors Voice by Bonnie Gillespie, this blog has taught me everything I needed to know about the show business. The Acting Blog by Mark Westbrook is a great no-BS blog on acting. I also love blogs like The Green Room blog, Backstage Unscripted, The Actors Enterprise, all written by actors for actors. A Younger Theatre is a great platform led by young people passionate about theatre, I learned a lot about UK's theatre scene through this website and its blogs and I'm lucky enough to write for them too - my blog is called International View. Or actor blogs like Stars In The Eyes, The Great Acting Blog or B.A.B.E. to name just a few, are a great source of inspiration and advice too.

Inspiration?

Actors who get things done, who take their careers into their hands and always work on mastering their craft no matter the level they're on.

Top tips for other bloggers

I'd say just start blogging and learn as you go. Read a lot of blogs to learn about formatting and SEO. Choose the design for your blog so it resembles your personality and the theme of your blog, as well as is pleasant for people's eyes and looks professional. Aim to improve, don't settle for what you are doing now thinking it's good enough. Always appreciate your readers and take the time to create relationships with them. You do it for them, after all, so be there for them. Find a targeted audience for your blog and write about what you know, don't try to just come up with something, write what you care about and are passionate about with the targeted audience in mind. Put yourself in their skin and ask yourself if what you are writing is going to give them something.

Do you make a living blogging?

- Not yet, but would love to as it would allow me to write more. Currently I'm looking into opportunities to do so.

Name: Catherine Balavage

Blog: Frost Magazine

How long have you been blogging for? Over ten years...gulp!

Describe your blog. Frost is a thinker's lifestyle magazine, a magazine for smart people who love fun. I also have an acting blog.

How did you get started? My love of reading lead to a love of writing

Highest point? Frost launch party, being picked up by Handpicked Media, covering everything from London Fashion Week to the Raindance Film Festival. Interviewing Zac Goldsmith and Alain De Botton.

Lowest point? The hosting company suspending my account because we were getting too much traffic. I had to move the site from one server to another. I had no idea what I was doing. Also: someone hacked the site and I lost some content.

Favourite blog? All of the above! And Hintmag and Feministing.

Inspiration? Every writer who ever inspired me to write my own stuff. My parents who told me I could do anything I wanted.

Top tips for other bloggers Do it because you love writing and have something to say. Don't do it just because you could pick up lots of free stuff. Also, listen to your instincts.

How do you make a living blogging? Affiliates and advertising.

Thank you for reading my book. I hope it helps and good luck with your blogging. Oh, and check out http://frostmagazine.com

OTHER BOOKS BY THE SAME AUTHOR:

How To Be A Successful Actor: Becoming an Actorpreneur

The Wedding Survival Guide: How To Plan Your Big Day Without Losing Your Sanity.

ABOUT THE AUTHOR

Catherine Balavage is a writer, editor and actor. She lives in London with her husband and their son.

Printed in Great Britain
by Amazon